WILLIAM
THE
CONQUEROR

WILLIAM
THE
CONQUEROR

By

Hilaire Belloc

TAN BOOKS AND PUBLISHERS, INC.
Rockford, Illinois 61105

ISBN: 0-89555-468-2

Library of Congress Catalog Card No.: 92-60959

Printed and bound in the United States of America.

TAN BOOKS AND PUBLISHERS, INC.
P.O. Box 424
Rockford, Illinois 61105

1992

The whole thing [the "conquest" of England] was over by 1074, and it is from that moment that we can best turn to consider the effect of all this on Europe and the west. It was undoubtedly greater already than William had envisaged, and it was to produce fruits far greater still...All this business from Hastings onwards is essentially the re-entry of Britain more fully and finally into the European unity of which of course it had always formed a part; and this showed itself in the ecclesiastical structure of the island, in the economic and political organization of it, in the unity which it founded based on one class of similar habits and speech—to be predominant in a hundred years from the Grampians to the Levant.*

—From Pages 62-63

---

*That is, from the hills of central Scotland to the lands bordering the eastern Mediterranean.—*Editor,* 1992.

Map of England and Normandy.

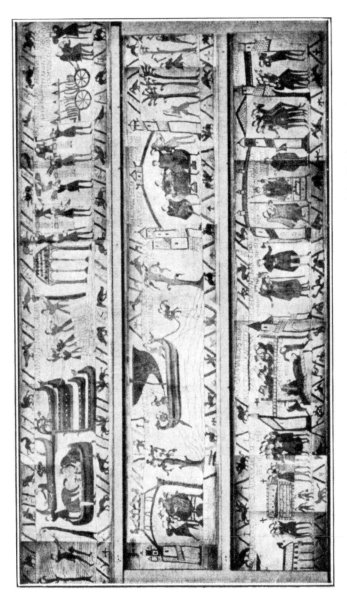

Preparations for the invasion of England; the death of Edward the Confessor; and the coronation of Harold. (*From the Bayeux tapestry, Victoria and Albert Museum*).

WILLIAM
THE
CONQUEROR

A short, broad-shouldered northern Frenchman, approaching his fortieth year, a man with long arms, powerfully built, and famous for the strength of his hands, clean-shaven, square-jawed, obese, vigorous—all that—decided, at about five o'clock of an autumn evening on a Sussex hill, the destinies of England and, in great part, of the world.

It was on the mile-long ridge where now the village and ruins of Battle stand, some half a dozen miles north of the sea at Hastings, that this man won the great fight. It was his intelligence, his will, his tenacity, which had done all. The hosts had seen each other first from opposing hills at morning, the action had hung quite undecided hour after hour, the sun was close on setting, when in that "last quarter of an hour," upon which Foch had said that victory depends, the line of the defenders broke and the charge of the attack poured through. All was at once mastered in the failing light; but until that final moment it lay even which of the swaying lines should first succumb to the agony and the strain.

This man was William, William the Bastard, Duke of Normandy, thenceforward to be King of England and the principal figure in the western world.

By what road had he reached this height?

A French woman of the petty bourgeois class, the daughter of a tanner, whose name is given as Harleva or Arletta, had borne him in the small dark thick-walled room of a great castle to a very young lover who was soon to be the ruler of all that land—Robert the Devil. There today you may see beneath the

1

castle wall in the valley far below the tanneries still at work upon the little stream.

The greatness of that child in his manhood caused legends to arise about this birth, and the tradition is strong that he was a child of great vigor, soon giving promise of coming energy. It is certain that his father (who became in his first manhood master of all Normandy, perhaps through a crime) saw in the little boy a successor who should have the strength to maintain the difficult unity of that land; for when the Bastard was but seven years old or so, probably early in the year of the Incarnation 1035, perhaps late in the year before, Robert the Duke, having a long journey to take very far away in obedience to a vow, set the boy before his nobles and had them swear that when he himself was dead they would hold the child as their lord.

And so they swore. Yet the young father had done nothing in those seven years to make him legitimate, as he might have done by canonical marriage with Arletta before setting forth, and this although he knew that one legitimate descendant at least of the Ducal line might later be put forward with a rival claim. He was determined that his own blood should rule, and so imposed it; and having done this went out as a pilgrim to the Holy Land and to the Sepulchre of the Lord. Some said that his strong determination to leave Normandy without a chief and in peril for so many months, to be cut off by so many hundreds of miles—half a year's marching—was due to a burning remorse. For Robert's brother Richard, who had been Duke before him, had died suddenly and after a reign very brief; therefore it was said in secret, but widely, that Robert was the author of his death and that Richard had died poisoned. Richard had died childless and Robert had other children, but he had thus fixed upon the very young boy William for his heir.

So he went out, but he did not come home. On the way back from the Holy Places, having come not a third of return, he fell sick and died—and he was still quite young—in the town of Nicea before the year was fully over. The bastard child stood alone.

Yet his title was admitted—perilously admitted, but admitted;

and for the dozen years through which he was to grow to manhood, though his guardians were murdered and though rebellion
was active or threatening all the time, his throne was held.

This was because there lay about the title of Normandy an
awe and majesty, founded by the continuous will of certain men
succeeding from father to son and by the accidents of time: and
now we must see what that world was into which the boy was
born, and why the oaths of the great when they swore to hold
him as Duke were of such effect.

More than five hundred years before the day in which Arletta
had given birth to Robert's child a slow change in the structure
of western Europe had at last matured. All the old world had
been, a thousand years before the boy's birth, one society—from
the plains of Asia to the Atlantic and from the Scottish mountains
to the Sahara. All that great sweep had been the Empire of
Rome, pagan, dominated by rich men who owned great multi-
tudes of slaves, alive with a very high civilization, splendid in
building and letters and arms. The soldiers of the Roman forces
ruled it, but without oppression; it had all become one, Greek-
speaking to the east of the Adriatic, Latin-speaking to the west,
and it had seemed under its Emperors to be eternal.

But it grew old. From pagan it slowly became Christian in
those first five hundred years, but it became Christian too late—
as St. Jerome mourned—for the fresh life of the Church to pre-
serve it as it was. A fatigue was upon it, and, having more effect
than that fatigue, a change in its tissue. The great army which
bound that huge body together, the army whose commander-in-
chief was also the monarch of all, had come to be more and
more recruited from the outer less civilized men from beyond
the frontiers of the Roman rule—Slavs, Moors, Arabs, Celts,
but especially Germans. These outer men were not the enemies
of Rome; they had been filtering into the higher civilization for
centuries as slaves, as free workers, as adventurers, even as
raiders. When they came as raiders, though always repulsed,
they left remnants of their bands behind, which added to the
less civilized elements of the Empire. But the chief effect they
had was on the military body, which was the governing part of

all that world. They had come in especially as hired soldiers.

When the fatigue of that old society had grown such that the Emperor could not collect his taxes nor directly administer distant districts through his officers, the gathering of the tribute and the governing of the various parts fell to the more vigorous of the army chiefs, especially those whose leadership was the stronger from having an hereditary character. These men who took over the local government and enjoyed its revenue still thought of the Emperor far off in Constantinople as the lord of their world, but they sent him no tribute and they were under no military orders of his.

The society over which they ruled, in the west at least, had also been transformed. The great owners of land and slaves were very slowly acquiring a private government of their own over the estates they possessed. Not only their slaves but their freemen began to regard them as lords. The thing went on for centuries. Men who were the owners of many villages, great through their wealth, became also great in power to rule. Lords who were owners of but one or two villages would often group themselves under a great man.

Some two hundred years before the life of this Bastard who was born at Falaise, the very slow, imperceptible process had become complete, and everywhere men spoke of Government as a matter of allegiance—a personal tie—and the idea of Imperial Government had disappeared. The lesser man's duty was to the greater man a duty of service, of fixed dues, and of following him for brief spaces in arms; the greater man's duty was of protection of those so bound to him. All the lordships of land throughout the west were of this sort. Those who had once been officials of the old Imperial system, commanders of its armed forces and administrators of its tribunals, called Dukes and Counts, were no longer military officers nor civilian officials, they were hereditary great lords of land bound together in a society which went upwards from the lordship of one village to right of rule over a whole province.

But while all this had been going on, Christendom—as the Empire had long become—was attacked from all sides, and nearly succumbed. An intense new heresy came in from the Arabian desert, Mohammedanism, soon appearing rather as a fierce new religion than as a heresy. It swept over the east and over Africa, over nearly the whole of Spain; it even raided into the heart of Gaul beyond Poitiers, though it was beaten back; and from the east and the northeast, pagans of every sort, not only civilized as were the Mohammedans, but as dangerous through their barbarism, looted and raided Christian Roman land. Christendom survived. In the west at least, where its rites were in the Latin tongue and its hierarchy organized under the Bishop of Rome, it began to press back the Mohammedan. They were expelled from Spain, and all over western Europe the heathen raiders also were tamed, absorbed, baptized. Christendom even went forward beyond its old boundaries in one field. It passed beyond the Rhine and extended its civilization into the Germanies. The generation of those who were old men when Arletta had borne her son had seen the beginnings of a spring: Christendom had begun to conquer again, the pressure was relaxed, the beginnings of a new Europe were founded.

Now this rising society into which William of Falaise was born was not a western Europe or Christendom divided into nations as we know them now. The great lordships had grouped themselves into provinces, which largely followed the lines of the old Roman divisions, and the heads of these provinces were independent monarchs, though few of them were called Kings. Thus in the north there was indeed a King of England, but also a Count of Flanders—monarch of the Low Countries and the northeast of France. A Roman division called "The Second Lyonesse" had become Normandy under its monarch, the "Duke," a word which had meant "General." Sometimes they called him "Marquis," which had meant a "Frontier Guard." Beyond, to the west, the Armoricans had made Brittany, also under its monarch, and in the center, round Paris, was the Duchy of France, and further to the south and east the Duchy of Burgundy. And then there was a mass and tangle of subdivisions, men acknowledging the rule of a monarch of a province but powerful within the boundaries of their own lesser territory; and everywhere the right to rule was not attached to certain frontiers or to any constitution, but was *personal*, the greater lord having a claim to the service of the lesser lord in an inextricable network of dues and rights.

But in what looks to us such confusion two things stand out firmly. First, the local monarchs of large districts, whether they were called Kings or only Counts or Marquises or Dukes, had no real superiors. Those of whom *they* were the superiors paid dues or service in arms, but they were free to help, or not to help, outside their own lands. Within those lands it was *they* who had taken over the revenues of the old Imperial Domain, the forests and the waste lands and certain towns; and many village estates, or lordships, were also concentrated in their hands. It was they who appointed to the principal offices of state, and to the bishoprics and great abbeys. To satisfy a sense of unity, to satisfy a vague feeling that over wide districts there was still something in common, these independent rulers would give the title of "King" to one of their number. They had so chosen the Duke of France to be called "King" over him of Flanders and him of Normandy and him of Brittany and the rest. But they remained their own masters.

And the second fixed principle throughout was the way in which property was arranged and wealth distributed and income gathered. This was all-important, for of this the structure of society was made.

The old Roman landowners from whom the nobles were descended would possess the area of a village or "Manor," having their own great house in the midst and the fields of the estate tilled by slaves as also by certain freemen, who were none the less bound up with the lordship of the land. In the course of centuries and under the slow influence of religion the slaves had become serfs: that is, they were not chattels to be bought and sold, but only bound to certain services. They were rooted upon their village land and had hereditary right to their homes from father to son, on condition that they did certain fixed works for the lord upon a portion of the village land which he reserved for himself, and that they paid him certain dues. Some few there still were when William of Falaise was born who could be bought and sold, as all slaves could have been bought and sold centuries before, but the number so remaining was small. Most men, though bound to their village lord and working for him, enjoyed the fruits of their own toil upon their own portions and also the common rights of pasture. The dues payable on a village, and the crops which the lord gathered on his own land, and his portion of the woods and all the rest of it, made of each village unit a supplier of income to the lord, and a village was said to be "worth" so much—meaning, not its total produce, but a much smaller amount, to wit, that part of the total produce which made up the lord's private revenues. It was upon this "worth" of each village that the whole structure of that society was built.

When a village lord died, his heir would take up the lordship upon payment of death-duties to his over-lord. The heir of this over-lord when he died would in turn pay death-duties to a superior lord, until the chain of payments stopped with the ruler of the whole district—the Count of Flanders, the Duke of Normandy, the Duke of France (who was also called "King"), the Duke or Count of Brittany, or the King of England.

The lordships were not all lay, many were ecclesiastical; the great bishoprics seated in the old Roman towns (in Normandy there were seven) were endowed with village revenues of this kind; they were lords, each of them, of so much land. The great monastic foundations were lords in the same way, and in the individual villages the priests were maintained by dues payable upon land set specially apart, and by tithes.

From this arrangement of society it came about that the monarchs of the various districts were by far the wealthiest men, for indeed wealth and government went together. And the greater lords with many manors and the many dues payable to them were far wealthier than the under-lords. At the bottom of the ladder of lordships were the lords of single villages; and below all lordships was the great mass of the tillers of the soil, serf and free, for much the most of that society lived on or by the land. There were towns, some of great size considering the times, there were flourishing ports, there were craftsmen and merchants, it was a very varied and active society; but the mass of it and the general economic structure of it was agricultural.

Now among these local monarchs Normandy, which the Bastard child was to inherit, had a character of its own. He of Normandy was of a special kind. For in Normandy the local power had established itself with a stronger organization than could be found elsewhere, and this was due not to a difference in blood, though there may have been some slight difference in blood between most of that district and Brittany which lay to the west of it and Flanders which lay to the east: nor was it due to a distinction in speech, though Normandy was wholly French-speaking, while half Brittany spoke a Gaelic dialect and quite half Flanders spoke a Flemish one. It was a difference in the way the rule of the Norman Dukes had been built up.

Normandy being that administrative division of the Roman Empire called at its origin the "Second Lyonesse," the name had dropped out of use these five hundred years and more. The way in which it had come to be a separate kingdom, standing independent like the others around it, was this:

It had formed part of the Duchy of France when certain pirate raids had come during the worst time of the pressure upon Christendom from the pagan far north, raiding England and the north-western coasts of France and Flanders as well. These troubles were long ago—they had ceased more than a hundred years before the Bastard child was born.

These pirates came in small bands of a few hundred men at the most, sailing up the rivers, looting the towns, torturing, killing, burning and destroying. For more than a century they worked thus over north-western Europe, doing evil in England, in Ireland, in all the north of Gaul; and small as were their numbers as compared with the millions of the settled population, the persistence of their attack upon an ill-knit society threatened to break it. They even besieged Paris, then a small town, though they failed to take it. They did every kind of damage along the Loire and the Seine and the lesser rivers of all the north. They came from the southern part of Norway and Sweden and from Denmark, and were called Danes or Dacians, Northmen or

Normans—all these names meant the same thing. Their motive was plunder: they came from barren lands to lands still full of wealth, and from pagan lands to lands Christian and with a tradition of civilization. Among their leaders was an adventurer who in his own country must have had a name something like Ralph or Rolph; you hear it in various forms—Rollo, Rosus, or what not. He had no particular authority, he was only a petty leader of men as wild as himself; but there came a moment which gave him opportunity, and there was something in him which enabled him to seize that opportunity after a fashion which no other of the very numerous headmen of those swarms had been able to do in any country.

In those days the local rulers had not grown to be independent. They were still appointed by the one chief monarch of Christendom, who made a man Duke of Burgundy or Count of Flanders at his will. They could still in theory be recalled in those old days and others appointed in their place. But they were growing more independent every day and leaving their power to their sons. Soon they would be hereditary monarchs, each over his province.

The head of western Christendom, whose rule was not over-strong, but who still bore the name of Emperor—he, or rather those about him, proposed a settlement whereby this head of a robber band should use his soldiery for the administration of the district round the mouth of the Seine, where he was at the time raiding. It was an arrangement on a model which had been tried over and over again with success: the settling as ruler, with confirmed powers, of one who, if he were not settled thus, would with his armed men continue to increase the chaos. The thing had been done in England, which had suffered more from these Scandinavian pirates than any other country; it had been done in Chartres and elsewhere. Long before that time it had been done in case after case where a turbulent soldier had been too much for the central power. The main thing in such settlements was the acceptation by the new chieftain of the Catholic Faith, and his practice of it signified his entry into the civilization around him. Rollo and those with him had come as pagans from the north. He accepted baptism, he married a daughter of the Emperor, and there was handed over to him to rule the basin of the lower Seine—that is, the Second Lyonesse—the capital of which was Rouen.

The province as a whole had six other bishoprics, the descendants and the representatives of the old Roman city districts. There was Coutances, and all that peninsula which projects into the Channel called the Cotentin; there was Sées lying to the south of this; there was Bayeux (in which long ago the Roman power had kept one of its numerous garrisons of hired German mercenaries, in this case a Saxon one, like most of those along this coast). There was Avranches. There was Lisieux, there was Evreux; as well as Rouen, the metropolitan see.

Rollo, thus finding himself a regular official of civilized society, became much stronger through the fact that such officials were everywhere becoming independent men, as I have described; for feudalism was in full growth. He could not at first extend the power seated at Rouen over the whole of what had been the Second Lyonesse, he could not enforce himself over the western part; but there is this remarkable difference between the district which he now governed with the title of "Marquis" or "Duke," that there was not below him, as below the others, a regular ladder leading up through the lesser lords of manors to their greater lords, and so to the first of them all, the monarch of the province. For some reason of which we know nothing, which may have had something to do with the break-up of order during the private raids, or may have been native to the place from long before, the Imperial lands, the "Domain," the village estates and forests, and the various rights and direct rulership over the towns passing to the Duke of Normandy with his appointment, bulked more largely by far than did the corresponding possessions of a Count of Flanders or a Duke of Brittany. And there had not arisen groups of numerous manors held by one man who should stand as over-lord between the smaller one-village lord and the great ruler of them all at Rouen.

The result was that the old Roman principle of monarchy, the putting of government under one will, was stronger here than anywhere else in Gaul. No doubt Rollo's own character had something to do with this. But of that again we know nothing. At any rate he seized upon the opportunity, and through a long succession from father to son that character of central rule was never lost. It was remarkable that in this province, which happened to take its new name from a few Scandinavian pirates who had but little affected its blood and who brought with them no institutions nor any ideas of organization, being barbaric, the best and most Roman organization should have appeared.

All this affair, whereby Rollo the Norwegian, or whatever he was, was set to be Governor of the Second Lyonesse, now to be called "Normandy," had become an old rooted thing long before this boy William was born to Robert in the castle of Falaise. Rollo had died an old man, a hundred years before William was born; no memory of paganism even among the few who had practiced it, or of northern speech even among the few who had clung to it after Rollo's time, remained. The place was wholly French, that is, Romanized, in law, custom, tradition, building, speech, cooking, writing—all civilization; and was even the strongest and most typical part of that civilization.

Into this Roman inheritance of monarchy Rollo's descendants fully entered. His son, who had for mother a sister of the Count of Senlis near Paris, confirmed all this; his grandson Richard gave still stronger proof of how rooted his Romanized idea of monarchy had become in Normandy, for William, Rollo's son, had died, murdered by his neighboring rival monarch, the Count of Flanders, and had left his boy Richard only ten years old. And yet Richard, though a child, was accepted, and had the longest reign of all the Norman Dukes, not dying till 996, by which time even the oldest man could not remember the time before Rollo had been established and the strict new state developed.

It was during this Richard's earlier youth that the last of those few who could remember the pagan customs and pagan tongue died out. Richard's son again, Richard II, whom they called Richard the Good for his piety (for all that house had become devoted to the Church, as being the very spirit of the civilization for which they stood), carried on the tradition; and by this time indeed there could be no question of its non-continuance.

Richard's daughter Emma, the sister of Richard the Good, was married to the King of England, Ethelred, just at the turn of the century, twenty-five years or so before William of Falaise was born. That marriage of the daughter of Normandy with the English King was to be the beginning of a great change, which ended in the uniting of Normandy and England. It was Richard the Good who had those two sons, Richard and Robert, of whom the first had so short a reign and was believed to have been poisoned or in some way got rid of by his brother, whose violence of reputation had got him that nickname of "The Devil."

Such was the child's descent; around him were many powerful lords all pledged to support his claim, and many loyally doing so. Most of them, clerical or lay, were what they were through having in them the blood of the Dukes: he was head of a widespread governing family as well as the head of the State. But his position was what I have called it—perilous—and that for a reason which may be misunderstood. The danger to the boy William in those years of his childhood was not merely that he was a child and therefore weak, for his guardians were men with retainers, they administered for him a vast, well-organized income, and all the machinery of what was by now the best arranged state in the north and west. No, the attack on the child proceeded from two sources: first, the jealousy felt for his guardians by equals who would not brook men like themselves enjoying greater opportunities; hence the conspiracies and quarrels among them leading to murder. But the other more important cause was the desire in almost every great lord of those days, especially of such as possessed so many lordships as to be able to command small armies of followers, to keep the Crown where it was but to keep it weak.

It was not a desire for mere independence—that would never have suited the book of a feudal noble unless he saw his way to carve out for himself a new monarchy—and that could only be done on a very large scale, or by a distant expedition, as to the Holy Land. Within his own provinces, what suited his book was to be as little controlled as possible, and yet to have at least a nominal chief, his allegiance to whom he could use as an argument against the encroachment of some outside power. Thus when William of Falaise was still a child, and all the time while he was still only a growing boy with no great personal authority (though he increased in this through his teens, for he was already of a masterful sort), such of the great as were not attached to his Court and got no advantage from his surroundings were the freer to encroach on domain land, to postpone their dues of payment, to find excuses against this or that service, and in general to enrich themselves. They were the freer to do all this so long as William's own weakness weakened the central government. For we must remember again that all ties then were personal; in early life the age, and later the character of a ruler, made all the difference to his real power; and this was true even in so well-organized a state as Normandy, with its strict system of accounts, its traditions of accurate survey and definition and its already fully formed body of local law.

But, while they took all the advantage they could of the child William's minority, the nobles stopped short of that which would either have broken up the State altogether, to their own loss, or—what would have been still worse for them—put in the active suzerainty of some powerful neighbor. In the long run they overreached themselves.

It must not be thought that because this peril was always present and occasionally active it was not a fine Court, with great wealth and all its habits surrounding the boy. His pride in these was increased by the connection of his family with the Crown of England; for though just over there beyond the seas a larger Christian land than Normandy had been thrown into perpetual confusion by the continuance of the pirate raids which on the Continent had been stamped out, though the social structure in England had been weakened to a point never reached south of the Channel during the heathen and half-heathen pressure of the dark time, the realm was a great one in the eyes of the Court of Rouen. If socially inchoate, it was wealthy, and though it was subject to smoldering civil war from the presence of many half-civilized Scandinavians in its midst, not only in the north and east but in London, and with a perpetual threat of aid from their pagan and half-christianized fellows from beyond the seas, yet it was a larger thing than Normandy and had behind it a very ancient tradition. The Church in England and the great monasteries helped to confirm this. Though there had been dreadful pillage and destruction during the pirate raids, still the great ecclesiastical foundations of England, with Glastonbury at their head, were famous enough throughout the western world, and an Archbishop of Canterbury was a greater man in the western Church than an Archbishop of Rouen—though not than an Archbishop of Rheims.

Now this most important realm of England lay close to the Bastard's experience as he grew up from early childhood into those formative years when a boy begins to know, most imperfectly but vividly, the world about him. Before he was born, Ethelred, the English King who had married Emma, the aunt of Robert, William's father, had died. Ethelred's son by an earlier marriage, Edmund, had also died; and the Scandinavians had effectively taken possession of London at least, under a little eager fellow, almost a dwarf and almost a genius, Canute. But that had not broken the boy's idea of intimacy between his own family and the realm of England, for Emma of Normandy, on Ethelred's death, had married Canute, the new King. Before William was born, Ethelred, in his first defeats by the Danes, had taken refuge in Normandy, and the elder and younger sons of Ethelred by Emma, called Edward and Alfred, would successively be the true heirs to the English throne, if ever the English should be rid of the foreign usurpers from beyond the North Sea.

These lads, twenty years older than their little cousin William, were brought up at his Court. They got everything from their mother and their mother's tradition. They were French in speech and manner, and the knowledge that England was theirs of right was ever present to those about them, and to young William himself. They were fair, gentle, timid; and Edward, the elder of them, had already a reputation for that special goodness which was to ripen into holiness.

At the very beginning of his life, just after his father's death, the little Duke had this claim of theirs vividly impressed upon him when he heard the story of their effort to take what was theirs by right, the Crown of England.

Edward had sailed to Southampton, but had been repelled: to Alfred a horrible thing had happened.

There was in the England of those days a man singularly strong in character and singularly evil; he bore the common name of Godwin, but he had become in the eyes of Englishmen a Dane. He had climbed to power (probably he was already of high birth and almost certainly possessed of lordships in the county of Sussex, with which it seems his father had had some connection of authority) by attaching himself to the foreign usurper Canute. He had shown courage and skill as a young man in Canute's foreign wars, and Canute had married him to the sister of his own wife's brother Ulf, a great Danish noble reputed (I think falsely) to be descended from a Bear. Godwin's foreign Danish wife bore him children, to whom he gave Danish names, and who inherited their father's character: Sweyn, the eldest, Harold, Tostig, and a daughter Edith, and others with whom we shall be less concerned.

It was wholly to the interest of this man Godwin, who at that moment of Canute's death was the most powerful person in the realm of England, to prevent the true heir from taking the throne and to see to it that the line should continue in the family of Canute—the family that had made him and would, traditionally, continue to increase him.

There was written (we may presume it was a forgery) a letter from Emma inviting the younger brother of Edward, Alfred, over to England on the chance of getting the throne now that Canute was dead. Alfred came. Godwin received him treacherously, as though he were supporting the true heir, brought him from Kent, where he landed, to his own town of Guildford, and there betrayed him to armed men who were followers of Canute's son Harold, the man who was Alfred's rival for the throne of England and had seized it. Thus fallen into the hands of his chief enemy, Alfred was treated with that cruelty for which the

Scandinavian pirates were detested throughout Christendom. He was ridden naked through England, his eyes were torn out, and he died of the mutilation—the more to confirm the son of Canute upon the throne.

This was the kind of news of England and of the factions tearing her which were the early and childish memories of William.

Now this Harold, the son of Canute (whom they called Harold Harefoot), the murderer (with his accomplice Godwin) of the gentle Alfred, soon died of his debauches. Here again was a chance for the true remaining heir, Edward, to come from the Court of Normandy and receive the throne of his fathers, and be crowned as they had been at Westminster. But Emma, now an elderly woman, who apparently had had in her life one great affection, that for her second husband Canute, did nothing for her elder son by Ethelred: she supported the claim of her second son by Canute called Hardicanute, and he was made King of England—yet another usurper in the place of a rightful king. But that usurper was half-brother to Edward, and he also was gentle, as the other son of Canute had been cruel and vile. He sent for Edward to come to his Court, and Edward came. As for Godwin, he had obtained a public acquittal of the accusation against him, and officially he was free to deny that he had betrayed Edward's brother to a horrible death—though men knew that it was true. But Edward thus at Court, gentle, and increasing in holiness, tolerated him, and more than tolerated him—may indeed have thought him innocent. So the masterful Godwin there remained, dominating that Court.

When his cousin Edward thus left Normandy, William of Falaise was some fourteen years of age—between thirteen and fourteen—and the character which was to impress its sincere but somewhat secret manhood upon all that time, its judgment and its power, were already forming. Within two years—William rapidly growing, not indeed to a tall stature but to great strength of body and understanding—Emma's son Hardicanute died in his turn, and there was no one with so immediate a right to succeed as the Norman-bred, the French-speaking modest Edward, already present in the Court. In that day when personality meant so much in a ruler, he had not a personality which could impress itself. His saintliness was justly admired; it endeared him to the people over whom he was to rule; but he was timid, very gentle, pale-haired (almost an albino, it is thought), and easily swayed (in matters where his conscience was not affected) by the worldly counsel of those around him; easily dominated by violence or tenacity of character in his immediate circle.

There was talk of yet another usurpation from among the Danes, but Godwin turned the scale. He decided for Edward. Here would be a king beside whom his own strength would be doubled. So Edward was crowned King of England at Westminster on the third of April, 1043: he was already some forty years of age. William of Falaise had thus a cousin overseas who was King, living in the traditions of the same Court as his father's uncle Ethelred had lived in; King of England, the very large island over against the northern shore. And in that England already there were men from Normandy holding places of power here and there, and their numbers increased. It was Emma's first marriage that had done this, and the superiority of the more ordered culture of the Continent: and especially a growing ecclesiastical connection, and all the memories of Ethelred's long sojourn in the Ducal Court and of Edward, now King, bound up with it.

In the first five years of his cousin's reign over England William attained manhood. His strong broad frame was formed, the sombre energy of his face—still youthful—was fixed; and a trial of strength must come between the great men of the Duchy who had so much of profit from a weak minority and him whom as a child they had maintained their lord, not for his authority but for the sake of their own freedom. Now that he was grown a man in his twentieth year it must be decided whether their claim should continue or his new and stronger rule should be affirmed. That was the issue. It was decided in a pitched battle, fought on slightly falling open ground east of Caen—the field of Val-ès-Dunes—and was decided by the army which Henry, the King of France and William's suzerain, brought in from the Duchy of France to the south. Henry, accepted as King by all these great states of the French, no stronger than some of his own vassals but having the authority of the title and being a new neighbor with force at his disposal, had been made guardian to William by William's father Robert before he had gone off to the Holy Land. The reason that the King of France came in to help the young Duke of Normandy at this turning-point of his story was not the bond made by this guardianship: it was rather the vital principle of monarchy. If the monarch of Normandy should be dispossessed or even disarmed by his feudal inferiors, by the great lords who owed him dues and service, then that which was vital to the order of the time, the strength of the great provinces and of their rulers, would be imperilled and there would be chaos. Later, when William had grown stronger still and almost seemed to overshadow his neighbor, the King—as Duke of France—resisted him and attempted to limit his power. But in this year, 1047, before as yet the Duke of Normandy had led his people in arms, while he was yet on the boundary between boyhood and manhood, his authority must be confirmed or the principle upon which government reposed would fail. That was the reason of the King of France's intervention at Val-ès-Dunes.

The campaign had been so ordered that William and Henry had happily to meet no enemies from beyond the Seine; the combination was made by the lords furthest from the seat of power of the government. They came past Caen, then a town with a growing market but not yet walled and never one of the ancient Gallic tribal centers nor one of the later Bishoprics; it was at a short march from Caen to the east along the Roman road that they took the shock. Even as the battle was joined they were weakened by division among themselves—it was the approach of the King of France that had done this, for it was now clear which way the fight would go. By the end of the day the young man was left wholly master of his Normandy; there still would be plenty of other local rebellions and fights and sieges of castles held by his feudal inferiors, and resisting him on the plea of some grievance, but his supreme position was never threatened again. And, as the day of Val-ès-Dunes placed him thus towards

the outer world, so it gave him strength within: he was henceforward confident.

With victory thus won and King Henry gone back into his
own land, there came within the next two years of this—his very
early manhood—the two human beings who were alone to affect
his spirit strongly, to be his permanent companions and to decide
the form of his life: one the woman whom he married, the other
the priest and statesman whom he most trusted and who survived
him to confirm his dynasty. The first was Matilda, the daughter
of his great and equal eastern neighbor, the Count of Flanders;
the second was Lanfranc of Pavia.

In order of time Lanfranc of Pavia came first. This great Italian had been born at least twenty years earlier than the man
who was to be his lord; he may even have been twenty-two or
twenty-three years older. He was of important birth in his own
city, his father having what they still called "senatorial" rank,
a considerable lawyer and a magistrate. He was already well-
trained and learned (he knew Greek, which was rare in those
days), and by profession a pleader in the courts: by all his incli-
nation a learner and a teacher, and still more an organizer; a
man of silent enthusiasm and of order; a sort of pillar.

He came north to teach up and down through France, and
ended at Avranches in 1039, being then himself well over thirty,
and William as yet but a child in his twelfth year. All the new
movement that was stirring in Europe was also in this man's
blood, the new strength of the Papacy, the new schools and their
disputes, the new gropings toward universal laws. It was a fruitful
coincidence that he should be there, destined to be of such Norman influence, just at the time when William was growing into
manhood. He was as yet but a teacher when, in his wanderings,
seeking "the poorest monastery he could find," he came to Bec,
on the upper waters of the Risle in the great woods east of the
Seine. It was a little place rising on the banks of the stream,
secluded in its valley; and there he found Herluin, the superior,
of a strength of character like his own and avid of reality.

He had served some considerable novitiate when, two years
before Val-ès-Dunes, in 1045, Herluin had him made Prior and

he was again at the head of a school. This school was to be a great and growing center—not only of learning, but of characters whom this chief character molded. Here, much later, was to come Anselm, and a Pope was to be among the scholars. But its fame was yet to come.

Already by the year 1048 Lanfranc was known throughout the Duchy, and the young Duke, fresh from the new strength of Val-ès-Dunes, was under the spell of it when he determined upon the marriage which was to have so profound an effect upon his life.

The singularity of William's character was already marked. His long fits of silence, especially after his passions of anger; his brooding, his lonely planning, combined with the vigor of his wrath. He was singular in nothing more than this, that, being such a man, he was even thus, in the strength of his youth, chaste; it was part of the strength of his will. And there went also with that strength of will a comprehension of religion which was at once personal and political. He was exact in observance, large in endowment, and he perceived how the further organization of that which had been, since the end of the old pagan civilization, the one constructive force in Europe—the Church—should be part of the structure of his State.

But between him and Matilda of Flanders there lay two obstacles, one much stronger than the other. The one, the stronger, was the girl's temper: the other was a canonical bar: they were [within] the prohibited degrees of consanguinity.

What blood relationship there was between them we have not the materials to discover. [See p. 27, note.] Her mother was Adela, sister to Henry the King of France—Baldwin the Count of Flanders, her father, having married Adela after the death of her first husband. Now that the first husband had been the brother of Robert the Devil, she was therefore the aunt by marriage of William, and Matilda, her daughter, might be called William's cousin after a fashion. But that was no canonical obstacle, because there was no community of descent. Whatever this canonical obstacle may have been, however, it was close enough to raise a scandal and to lend weight to the attitude of the hierarchy and the Pope himself. There may have been some political element in this, some desire to prevent a yet closer relationship between the two dominant houses of the northern French coast—Flanders and Normandy—but this is unlikely, for the links made by such marriage were already numerous and formed a close network.

At any rate, on the plea of consanguinity, the marriage was clerically forbidden. The Pope next year, holding the Great Council of Rheims, formally and publicly declared the ban against such a marriage. That could be defied, and later was defied [See p. 27, note.]; Lanfranc, strict supporter of the law, joined in the denunciation, and later, William, in an explosion of anger, looted the fields of Bec.

But still, it was the young woman herself that most stood in his way. She had of her own initiative attempted a marriage with one of the great English nobles from the Severn valley, he had rejected her, and her anger had been published abroad. It is perhaps on this account that we find her, after the Conquest, possessed of this man's land. When she heard in her family that young William of Normandy was seeking her she made it an occasion for insult, recalling his bastardy with a jeer. His answer laid the foundations of the marriage. He rode off eastward with a few companions, came to where she was in one of her father's palaces (perhaps at Lille), and there was a scene of violence between them. In the most vivid of the various traditions it has left, the story is told of the young man coming in unannounced from the door of the great house in Lille, pushing into the room where she was, throwing her to the ground, knocking her about and making as plain as he could the effect which her comment had had on him. There he left her without more words; and after that she was determined that he should be her husband.

Four years were to pass before he was to obtain her; when he did so it was still in spite of the ecclesiastical ban and in defiance of it.

Meanwhile in England those first years of Edward's reign had bred what was inevitable, considering the characters of Godwin and of the King and the background of those civil wars and alien barbaric invasions of a realm dominated by three or four great families, half kings over their shifting districts, "the Earls." There had come a trial of strength between Godwin's ambition, with its hated Danish inheritance, and the new Court of Edward.

Godwin's sons were growing up; the most remarkable of them, the second, Harold (with his Danish name), in his early twenties; the eldest and worst, Sweyn (with his Danish name); Tostig, the younger and perhaps the most malicious (with his Danish name). They were a close clan. In the strength of himself and his sons and the forces he could levy, Godwin aimed at complete power. Opposed to him were the other great Earls, who feared (justly enough) that if he gained complete domination, what they had would be taken from themselves and their sons and given to the sons of Godwin, who already, with their father, directly governed the greater part of England. Godwin had also made his daughter, Edith, Queen. He had married her to Edward.

There were opposed to this towering and usurping figure three forces: first, the friends of the remaining rival Earls whose families still held land not yet absorbed by Godwin's half-Danish clan; there was secondly the strong popular feeling in favor of the holy King; and there was thirdly the King's private group of friends and those whom he had advanced. These were largely drawn from the better organized and more advanced surroundings of his youth; he had appointed to three of the great bishoprics three Normans, and one of them especially, Robert of Jumièges, being Archbishop of Canterbury, was the natural leader against the men who threatened to become by force the masters of England. Godwin had already imposed the pardon of his eldest son, who had been exiled after abominable crimes and whose murder of his cousin had made him detestable; and it had to come to a trial of strength.

The occasion was a petty one. The King's brother-in-law, the Count of Boulogne, was leaving England in 1051 after a visit when there was a fight in the streets of Dover between his retinue and certain men of the town. The King insisted that the town should be punished. It lay in Godwin's great earldom of the south; Godwin was therefore charged with the duty. He refused, by way of challenge. But he had miscalculated. All popular feeling was with the King; the remaining independent Earls joined large forces to the King's own. Godwin and his sons could not withstand them, and they fled, some to take refuge on the Continent, but Harold in Ireland, whence he set out to ravage the coasts of England in the old piratical fashion. Godwin's daughter, the Queen, was sent away from Court.

It seemed as though the forces of order had won, and during that lull the young Duke of Normandy made the chief political decision of his life. He crossed the Channel in great state to visit his cousin the King of England.

It was the latter part of the year 1052, perhaps at the end of the summer or in the early autumn, and it was William's first sea-faring. There was nothing of adventure nor even of high relief in that momentous journey, it was nothing of an expedition. Had it or had it not behind it any conscious plan? We must conclude that William already envisaged, however vaguely, the reversion to himself of the throne of this country. To understand his mood we must get into the minds of the men of that time, as of William himself, and not test the situation by genealogical tables alone—still less by modern nationalism, a sentiment inconceivable to the men of the eleventh century.

England presented to the contemporaries of William and Edward a province of Christendom which had surged and tumbled, during all living memory before Edward's accession, in a sort of chaos. It had been overrun by small but fierce and paralyzing heathen armies; it had been made the sport of their descendants even when those descendants had, very tardily, accepted Baptism and entered into civilization. There was no unity or security in the throne, there were no roots or tradition of successful government. The houses of France, Flanders, Normandy and Brittany were ruled by families unbroken for two hundred years and stretching back to the great Carolingian time—bridging, as it were, the darkness of the ninth century and springing from it. But England had been made the spoil alternatively of foreign half-civilized kings; the succession of the native house had been disturbed and unable to follow a fixed rule of inheritance, so that the opportunity had been given to the more powerful men, time and again, to choose as king whomever they chose to set up.

Moreover, unity within England was lacking. The very great houses had set themselves up as rivals to the throne—the Earldoms; and though not always their persons, yet their very title was Scandinavian and an anomaly. Also their boundaries shifted, and there would be sudden clashes and divisions.

When ten years before, while William was still a child, that native King Edward had at last been enthroned once more at Westminster, he was a King from overseas, he was Norman in all that counted—speech, manners, tradition, everything: and he was of such a temperament that the instability of the realm—if realm it could still be called—was made the greater by his presence. The few magnates, with their enormous wealth and power to levy independent armies, thought only of themselves; none more than Godwin, and Godwin counted almost as a Dane. Almost any strong candidate for the succession to such a state of things would have seemed normal enough to the time.

But the candidature of William was especially normal.

It must by now have been a familiar truth that Edward could have no heir; William was not only his cousin, but his most prominent living relative and the relative of the old lady Emma, with her enormous possessions and all the part she had played in the successive ambitions of rivals—the King's mother and William's aunt. She came right from the Norman blood; she was a half-man, *virago,* sprung from those men who had made the unity of Normandy. And Edward himself was part and parcel of the same Court, of the same social atmosphere and manner. It was certain that when Edward should die—and he was not a vigorous man, and he a quarter of a century older than the young Duke—the succession would lie between that young Duke and a family which had no right whatsoever, mere powerful rebels against whom equals would be in perpetual conflict. Nor was this French civilization which thus impressed itself upon all at the time a thing peculiar to Normandy, it was the air of all the north and west of Christendom. It was not only Edward's being virtually a Norman, it was more his being a member of that northern French civilization—as was the house of Paris, the house of Maine and the house of Flanders and the house of Boulogne. All that was needed to clinch the claim was some definite act, something that could be put on record.

William, in the course of his journey, obtained that act: he cannot but have aimed at it more or less consciously when he set out to visit the Court of his cousin. This act was some conditional promise of the succession made by Edward to William.

The value of such an act at such a time was of overwhelming weight. The rules of succession, nowhere absolutely fixed, were crystallizing towards their final shape of an exact heredity—the indisputable right of the elder male succession. But that had not yet come. And there was also crystallizing another tendency connected with the same idea of the sanctity attaching to kingship—a tendency regarding the kingship as a sort of property. The universal vigorous feudal ideas made for that, for the very essence of feudalism was the identification of ownership with rule. If, then, he who wore the Crown could have no heir, it seemed of right that he would leave it to him whom it would best fit, and no one could be fitter for that gift than a close relative who was of the same nurture, speech, manner, everything, and whose family was bound in with the English Court ever since Ethelred had married the daughter of Normandy.

This promise by Edward to William of the reversion of the English Crown became public property throughout Christendom; it formed part of the way in which the house of Flanders—closely connected both with Westminster and Rouen—looked at the world around them; it had the moral sanctity of the time behind it, and seemed at that time the normal development of the situation.

Young William arrived in great splendor with many of his lords about him: he came to a Court from whence the principal rebel, Godwin, had just fled in terror, with all the other magnates of the nation combined against him, he and his sons scattered, and those sons burdened with a most evil reputation for piracy and rapine, of which English men and women had been the victims. When William came he would further find men of his own kind established everywhere: they were in the principal Bishoprics, they held one of the Earldoms, they commanded certain garrisons. For a very long time past the influence of the widespread culture south of the Channel had impressed itself more and more to the north of it.

When therefore the Duke of Normandy returned to his country after his splendid journey, he was—in his own eyes and the eyes of his great equals to the south and west and east, also to the King of England himself, and we know not how many of the magnates of England—the heir to the throne. Had the succession fallen open soon after, had the frail Edward died in middle age instead of lingering as long as he did, William's claim might have been unquestioned. Confirming it would have gone not only a growing mass of stories, some probable, some improbable, but his own continued success in the confirmation of his kingdom and the spectacle of Normandy as the strongest of states.

It is disputed whether or not a public council in England confirmed the succession to William; the thing is affirmed clearly enough, but there are also affirmed in various forms other corroborative details, some of which are doubtful and others by their circumstances obviously legendary. At any rate, there you have William of Falaise by the end of 1052, still in the vigor of his very early manhood, established as the successor apparent to the English throne.

On William's return to his own place, that marriage upon which he had determined, that object which he had pursued with the tenacity and the power of waiting which, in spite of his youth, was already so marked in him, was obtained. The young woman had insisted upon it; her father, the great Count of Flanders, came across the Somme with his retinue to the frontier town of Eu in the next year, 1053, and in defiance of the ban which Leo the Pope had issued, the marriage was sealed.

The clergy still protested, and it was at this moment that William in his anger ravaged and looted the land of Bec and drove Lanfranc for a moment away. The metropolitan, the Archbishop

of Rouen, William's relative, who had an evil reputation but was of great political as well as of supreme ecclesiastical position, led the opposition. William called a synod of Normandy and drove him out, putting another and better man in his place. The quarrel with Lanfranc was short-lived, that powerful figure returned, and henceforward determined to be on William's side. He pleaded long for the removal of the papal prohibition. From Leo this could not be obtained, but in the next year that great Alsatian died, and it was not till five years after, in 1059, that Nicolas II, who had been a subject of Baldwin's, lifted the ban.*
With William's marriage there came not only the influence that was to support and direct nearly all the rest of his life, but that full relationship with the closely interknit ruling names of the time by which alone we can understand what his policies were and what therefore led up to the union of Normandy and England at last.

For it is essential, if we would comprehend that very long-past day, to forget the modern ideas of nationalism. What counted then was not language, still less the much vaguer conception of race in a Christendom which was one in religion and in social habit. What counted was those "monarchies," as I have called them, presiding over the great divisions of the north and west, Normandy, Flanders, the Duchies of France and Burgundy, England; and the leading figures in those monarchies. Now those leading figures form one close web of relationships, very intimate, and it is these that we must appreciate. William in marrying Matilda had married the daughter of the King of France's sister, the daughter of his aunt by marriage, Adela; for Adela

---

*With regard to the Church's laws against marriages between relatives: Some of these prohibitions are based on the natural law, and therefore the Church has not the power to dispense from them (e.g., the case of marriage between brother and sister). She does have the power to dispense from her own Church laws prohibiting marriage between certain more distant relatives. The case of William must have been of this latter sort.

After the legitimization of their marriage, William and Matilda consented to found two abbeys at Caen in penance for their earlier contumacy.—*Editor,* 1992.

was the wife of Baldwin of Flanders. All this criss-cross of relationships formed a compact set of personal interests in which Baldwin of Flanders, now William's father-in-law, holds the central position: to be guardian of the son of the King of France, Philip, later himself to be King; arbiter at one moment in the quarrel between the claimants for the English succession; and the power which tipped the scale at the end in favor of William.

For William by his marriage with Matilda was not the only man who put himself into close relations with the great ruler of the Low Lands. Godwin, who even more after his death than during his life was the true opponent of William, came closely into touch. It was at Baldwin's Court that Godwin took refuge during his exile after the enormities of his sons, and Godwin's son Tostig married one of Baldwin's daughters, the sister of William's wife Matilda. By a later accident Tostig came into conflict with his brother Harold, and was therefore a support to his brother-in-law William. But that was for the future; none could guess it then. For the moment one could only say that the house of Godwin, with the traditions of the hated Danish invaders, and the house of Normandy, which was William, were both looking for support to Baldwin's house of Flanders.

At the end of this same year, 1052, which had seen William at the English Court and his return from it, came Godwin's opportunity. He had already made one attempt to return, and had failed: he now made another, that succeeded. He had gathered great forces in ships and in men. When he reappeared in the Thames, the King's Court could send against him nothing stronger, and at that moment appeared the go-between who settled the whole affair, earning thereby the permanent gratitude and protection of Godwin and his sons. But it was an overreaching. They had better have kept away from such an ally! This man was one Stigand, a climber as Godwin had been, and a climber as Godwin had been through friendship with the alien conqueror Canute; but he was not of Godwin's caliber, and he was a much meaner man. He was a cleric, and he first appears endowed by Canute immediately after his victory over the English at Assendun to serve the church which Canute had built there in memory of his conquest. Thence he had advanced, putting larger and still larger revenues into his pocket, and holding at this moment the great bishopric of Winchester. He it was who passed between the one group and the other and made possible the return of Godwin and his sons—even of Harold, steeped in English blood from his massacre at Porlock and his ravaging of the English coasts.

This man Stigand could not but be further advanced. The price he demanded for his services was of the highest kind. The Archbishop of Canterbury—and the ablest and greatest of Godwin's enemies—had fled overseas. It was not as a Norman that he was turned out, for another great Norman, the Bishop of London, remained; it was only as the chief of Godwin's opponents. That he should have saved his life by exile when Godwin thus triumphed in no way affected his rights to the See of Canterbury; he was the duly established Archbishop, consecrated, enthroned and holding the Pallium. But Godwin insisted upon thrusting into that place the unlearned, the unpopular, the base Stigand. It was not only a monstrous appointment, but one made in the face of all that Christian opinion then was and in the very height of the returning tide, when strict Church law was being particularly emphasized. It was a challenge, and an insolent one.

But Stigand must be paid, and paid he was, not only by the Archbishop but by the revenues of the great monastic houses— Glastonbury, Ely, St. Albans. He put them all in his pocket. After all, he could not tell how long the luck would last!

The man was so blown upon that even those with whom he had struck the bargain hesitated to admit his powers as Archbishop; the clergy looked at him askance. The Papacy, of course, vigorously refused to admit his claim. Harold did not depend upon him for the consecration of his endowments, nor even would he consent to be crowned by him when the time for his own usurpation came.

I have called it "an over-reaching." Godwin and his house had over-reached themselves in the use they made of Stigand, and still more in the price they paid for that use. The Church and its laws, its spirit, and their infringement thereof were of such moment throughout Europe that scandal of this kind was a millstone round the neck of its authors.

William, away in Normandy, appreciated to the full what had been done: it was henceforth maneuver and watching between Godwin's house and his own. He appreciated the indignation of all Christendom against Stigand, and with that tenacity of his which knew when to be silent, he stored it up against the day when such forces could be used.

Godwin himself immediately died, and in the opinion of his contemporaries, which may have been superstitious but was certainly significant, he died as an example of the wrath of God. He fell in a fit at a banquet at the table of the King upon whom he had newly imposed himself, and men told each other so widely that it became of universal acceptance that he had so been struck down after an allusion by Edward to the mysterious death of his brother Alfred. Godwin had passionately protested, and hoped his food might choke him if he were guilty, whereupon his food so acted and he fell.

There followed a decade during which William of Normandy still further consolidated and increased his power. In the petty wars which now the Duchy of King Henry to the south would wage against him, now his own subjects, aggrieved and resisting in their castles, he always succeeded. They were the note of the day everywhere; the forces engaged were often small, the struggles were never decisive, nor attempted to be decisive save as to the fate of single individuals, but the string of his successes made him even more the master of the land than he had been in the first years after Val-ès-Dunes, or just before his marriage, when he had subdued one relative in the castle of Arques near Dieppe, another more distant on his frontiers at Eu, and had deposed yet another by the action of the ecclesiastical synod at Rouen.

A strong tide was flowing under William and bearing him on to fortune. With every year his power, his revenue, his prestige increased, and this tendency to rise continually before Europe was advanced by the general spirit of the time.

It was the moment when the word "Norman" was taking on

a higher significance; the power of the triumphant Norman adventurers in south Italy had shaken all Europe and was to ally itself with the reinforced Papacy, for it was the moment of the restoration of the Papacy and the great Cluniac reform, the purging and consolidation of the Church. The genius of the monk Hildebrand, later to be the great Pope St. Gregory VII, was urging on all western Europe in its uprising towards a renewed civilization.

William was identified with all this. He was, of all the monarchs of the west, the one most closely bound to the new order of the Church, and his link was through Lanfranc. The greatness and the fame of Lanfranc, moreover, and therefore of the Norman name, was supported by his struggle against that which inevitably accompanies a great intellectual revival—the beginnings of a heresy. Lanfranc appears as the opponent of Berengarius.

Berengarius of Tours had set out to rationalize the Sacrament of the Altar and to reduce the conception of the Real Presence. Lanfranc was the conspicuous and triumphant protagonist in favor of the ancient and unbroken tradition, it was during these years that he affirmed himself the champion of that to which Christendom was unalterably attached, and his personal force, mixed with the multitudinous power of the time, checked, threw back and defeated the assault of Berengarius and his clan. The denial of the Real Presence was not to be repeated until the Black Death had struck medieval society its mortal blow three centuries later. The victory of Lanfranc over Berengarius was won in those mid-years of the century, in the fifties, at Vercelli, at Tours and at Rome itself.

On the death of Stephen, who had succeeded his patron and cousin the great St. Leo as Supreme Pontiff in March, 1058, those forces which were making against the increasing vigor of reform and Hildebrand's energy proposed, and by a minority vote elected, a candidate to whom they gave the title of Benedict. Those who resisted had to fly from Rome, and Hildebrand was absent. A new and full choice under his direction established the canonical Pope, Nicholas II, before the end of the year, and in the following January the anti-Pope was driven out. Under the short new reign was organized the system of regular canonical election which so strengthened the new Papacy, giving it as it were a constitution and a rule of succession, so that the efforts made in Germany to undo all this failed. These successes of Hildebrand, who gave its driving power to the whole movement, were intimately mixed up with the new strength of the Normans in Italy and were bound through Lanfranc to the Duchy itself and to William.

To Nicholas II Alexander II succeeded, companion and intimate of Hildebrand and a Cluniac as Hildebrand was. Under him the German opposition was thrust still further back, its anti-Pope Honorius defeated, and the Papacy still further strengthened—and with it, as an ally, the Norman power.

But of all William's personal achievements at this time one stands out, both as a type of what was to come and as an extension of his own power—it was the conquest of Le Mans and of its district, Maine. Here, since we are approaching the great business of William's life, we must understand what was meant by that operation in order that we may understand what was to be meant by the much greater affair of Hastings and the English crown.

There did not exist in those days among Christian men the conception of right based upon force. Conquest in that sense, mere seizure of land and revenue by superior strength—that is, mere robbery—no man would have pretended to. One might thus seize by strength land and revenue which the Mohammedans had appropriated without right from its Christian owners, and by an extension of this doctrine it was admitted that the leader of armies might seize the pagan or uncivilized territory and impose upon it the system of Europe and its faith; but modern ideas of spoiling and sovereignty were unknown. Of spoil in goods and ransom after a victory there was plenty, but the doctrine that mere superior strength gave a title to possession was not in the mind of the day—it belongs to our own. No doubt a covetous man would have a wrong motive in pleading a right, but plead a right he always did, and unless he had done so he would not have been tolerated among his fellows. Now the extension of Norman power over Maine fell thus:

Maine, which marched with Normandy, and was the district to the south and west of it, largely in custom and manners an extension of the Duchy, was held in singular fashion. The local petty feudal monarch or Count had some part of the civil power and was the nominal head, but the Bishop (who was everything in the capital—Le Mans—and Le Mans was, one might almost say, as important as all the rest of Maine, the center and the rationale of its existence) was not appointed by the Count; he depended directly upon the King of France; and all the while the powerful neighbor of Anjou, and the family of Fulk who ruled here, claimed a voice in the affairs of Maine. The influence of the Bishop Gervaise was removed by the King of France, making him Primate of all Gaul as Archbishop of Rheims. Herbert, the Count of Maine, in fear of such powerful neighbors, commended himself to William for protection. A treaty was made whereby he was to marry William's daughter, one of William's sons was to marry his sister, and if the succession should fail it should revert to the Duke of Normandy. Herbert died, and William of Falaise at once insisted upon his claim. He made a proclamation that he would shed no blood, that he desired peace, and all that he required was his right: he entered and garrisoned Le Mans, overcame one stubborn center of resistance at Mayenne, and thus, in one stroke as it were, in the year 1063, had enlarged the district of his rule and the mass of his revenue and his recruiting field by nearly one-third.

While William Duke of Normandy was thus growing greater and greater, a now towering man throughout the west, England fell into further and worse distractions. The rule of St. Edward was not challenged, but that gentle holy man was overshadowed more than ever by the spirit and descendants of Godwin dead, with his legacy of crime, uncertain title, usurpation and civil war. It was now that Godwin's second son, Harold, succeeded to the place, but not the single dominations of his father.

He was a tall, strong, courageous young man just turned thirty; of an easy approach, as unscrupulous as were all the

Godwin blood, and as eager for gain. Hardly was his father dead when in that same Easter of 1053 he became as though by hereditary right Earl, which meant viceroy, over Wessex, and the process began whereby he was to be, without title, the chief power in England, and with him his brothers (and his sister, be it remembered, was Queen). Two years later his younger brother Tostig was put over Northumbria—so the north and the south were now both in the hands of Godwin's house.

But between those two dates, in the year 1054, there was taken by the holy King, apparently upon his own initiative, a step which might have been of the greatest moment. When Edmund Ironside had died in 1017, thirty-seven years before, and power over England seized by an usurper—the alien and invader, Canute—it was planned that the dead man's children, who were but babies, two sons, should be killed. That was in the true tradition of the Danish invaders. They were sent overseas for that purpose, but those who should have committed the crime took pity on them, and they were sent for protection far off to the holy King of Hungary, Stephen. One of them died, but the other, Edward, grew up in that distant land. To Edward then, now a man in his thirty-eighth year, who was by right of succession the heir to the childless King of England, Edward that King sent, with some pomp, in the year 1054. Against such a man, of the English blood royal, nephew of St. Edward and plainly holding the right to the succession should he be present, William, with whatever conditional promise he held, could claim nothing. Still less could the all-powerful house of Godwin and the ambitious Harold attempt to pass him over by any violent usurpation. Against the natural claim of the exile, now on his way home, the Duke of Normandy could and would do nothing; nor did he. But Harold was there, as real master of England, present at the heart of things, and it would be under Harold that the "Aetheling" would find himself.

What followed was strange. Edward the exile, the Aetheling, clearly hesitated in face of the peril before him. He tarried as long as he could upon his journey, waiting months at Cologne; it was not until the third year after the original summons had come that he landed in England with his little son, Edgar. During the very brief time that he yet had to live, though in England, someone arranged that he should not meet his uncle, the King. And at the end of those few weeks Edward the Aetheling suddenly died, and was buried in Old St. Paul's. It was inevitable that suspicion should fall upon Harold: but we have no proof. From that moment there was within the realm itself no obstacle to Harold's ambition, save the conditional promise upon which William of Normandy relied, for the little child, Edward the Aetheling's son, no one considered; in such turmoils no child could be king. By one account the promise to William was renewed and confirmed upon the Aetheling's death.

But Harold was in possession. By the end of the year he had added to his revenues the Earldom of Hereford, which had been held formerly by Edward's nephew, the son of his sister; and Harold's brother, Gyrth, was given East Anglia. With the other brother, Tostig, in the north, nothing but the central counties was not directly in the hands of Godwin's house. To strengthen Harold's position there was an attempt to regularize the false Archbishop Stigand, whose intrusion into the See of Canterbury the Papacy had utterly refused to acknowledge. Now St. Leo, the great and strong Pope who had thus stood out against the false position of Stigand, was dead; and in the year 1058 (which may also be the date—it is uncertain—of a voyage made by Harold himself to Rome) the pallium, a little woolen stole, the sacramental symbol of Papal recognition—that which would have made Stigand Archbishop indeed—was claimed and granted from Rome.

But once again the house of Godwin had over-reached itself. The pallium was sought and obtained from that brief irregular tenant of the Papal throne, Benedict X, who was (as we have seen) immediately to be turned out by the canonical elected candidate, who became Nicholas II. Henceforward, therefore, Stigand's position was worse than ever. He had the pallium indeed, the mark and consecration of the Primacy, but he had it from a man who had stood for opposition to all the new movement in the Church. Benedict X is hardly reckoned in the list of the anti-Popes, for he had not been set up after the election of another, but morally he counted as such, and Stigand having taken the pallium from such a man offended the opinion of Christendom even more than he had done by all his earlier irregularities. The chances of a more successful usurpation by Harold grew less, for now Stigand, Harold's ally, was more discredited than ever. Already there was the atmosphere of schism and of challenge to the rest of Christendom in the position of Harold and his unadmitted Primate.

In the year 1064 the situation took on a further development which was to be of the highest consequence. As is so often the case in this story, we are again not certain of the date; but 1064 is the most probable year in which to place the action which follows. It could hardly have been earlier, for in the year before, Harold was occupied in a laborious Welsh campaign; it could hardly have been later, because in the succeeding year the troubles in the north had begun.

This development, which was to be of such moment, came through a voyage upon which Harold then set out in the Channel, sailing from his own port of Bosham toward the French shores. What followed has been very variously described by different men at different dates writing in widely separated places, but much of the story is certain, and its whole historical point— Harold's fealty to William and promise to support his claim—is the most certain thing of it all. But there is discrepancy upon details, some of them important details, and our best plan for judging these is to follow the man who was on the spot, who was acquainted with and spoke to eye-witnesses of what happened, who knew William well and was his chaplain and historian, William of Poitiers.

Under such provisos, that most important happening must be told. Harold's motive in taking the sea was probably some negotiaton for hostages of his own family who were in William's custody; the voyage may even have been undertaken (though that is improbable) with the object of conveying a resolution taken at the English Court in favor of William's claim. At any rate, running too far before what was presumably a strong westerly wind and being unable to make a Norman port, Harold's ship took the ground in that wide bay of St. Valéry from which the Conqueror was so soon to sail with his centuries of ships in arms for England. Harold's ship was wrecked on that eastern shore of the bay where you may still see, from time to time, the timbers of boats that have got embayed and tried to beat out against the violence of the south-west wind; for it is shoal water. He had tried apparently to take refuge in the narrow and too shallow creek where the little stream called Maye comes in, the stream which rises on the battlefield of Crécy not many miles away. Now by law and custom, not only all wreckage fell to the local lord of the shore on which the wreck took place, but wrecked sailors were his also to hold for ransom. This district just east of the Somme was the county of Ponthieu (from the "*pontes,*" the bridges whereby the Roman road from Boulogne crossed the broad valley of the Authie). Guy was its lord, and Guy, exercising his right, kept Harold safe in his castle of Beaurain. His natural expectation would be that the ransom should come from Harold's own estates in England, some of the riches of which were only just across the sea in Sussex.

But William of Normandy acted at once. He was at hand to furnish what was required, and what was more, he was a neighbor whom this under-lord, though in no direct feudal relation with Normandy, would do well to favor. So Guy, lord of Ponthieu, handed over Harold, not without magnificence, to William in his frontier town of Eu, wherein it was customary to receive embassies from the east and where it will be remembered William had also received his bride. Guy of Ponthieu got wealth and landed endowment from William in ample recompense to console him for his loss of ransom from England; and Harold went off with William to the Norman Court, where he was treated, as his very high position rightly demanded, almost as an equal and with courtesy and splendor. He could of course, although he had not yet been present there, move in that Court with ease, for he had been at a French-speaking Court—that of King Edward—all his life, and so far as we can judge from the way things went, he went down very well, his tall figure, good looks, vivacity of speech and amenity of manner in the midst of those short broad-shouldered men, and his long moustaches contrasting with their severe clean-shaven faces. William knighted him, and took him as a companion in arms on a raid into Brittany—but the chief matter of all this hospitality and chivalry was Harold's oath of allegiance. It was a triple bond: there was not only the oath of allegiance whereby Harold became William's "man," just as William himself had become Edward's "man" in that long-past visit of his youth, but there was a solemn promise of marriage made by Harold to William for one of his younger daughters when, presumably, she should be of marriageable age. There was thus to be alliance between him and his new lord; further, there was a promise binding Harold by a solemn oath that he would support William's claim to the throne of England.

It is of the first importance if we are to understand what followed that we should grasp which of all this was the essential in the spirit of the time. The essential was the homage done to William. Because we today still have dynasties, we are inclined to insist upon that one of the points which is most comprehensible to us—the promise to support William in his claim to the English throne. But to the men of the eleventh century, it was Harold's homage to William, from which such a promise would naturally follow, that was the essential thing. Homage we no longer have, and on that account we tend to misunderstand the position. Of the many things that had put Harold wrong with the sense of Christendom, his breach of faith in this matter of homage was far the most serious. He had become William's "man," and yet he later not only acted directly against William's interests, but took the very place which he had promised, so far as he could, to secure for William himself. According to the conceptions of that day the very least a decent man could do would have been to stand aside. What he did actually do seemed monstrous, and, added to the other very grievous business of Stigand, and the wretched example which the whole career of Godwin and his sons had set before Europe, made the cup of opinion run over; so that Harold, when he later seized the throne, was already lost in the conscience of Christendom.

Harold returned to England, and the next thing he found was yet another piece of chaos wrecking the unfortunate country. This time it was his brother Tostig who had started the trouble. When Tostig had been made Earl over Northumbria, that is, master of the north, it was part of the plan for putting the house of Godwin with Harold at its head in mastery over England. But the violence and ambition of Godwin's sons made so simple an idea as family alliance work ill. Tostig was intolerable to the Yorkshiremen, his harshness and tyranny drove them to rebellion; they massacred to a man his personal guard of two hundred, and having the support of the two young men who were the sons of the dead Earl Aelfgar—he who had been the only great local ruler outside the Godwin clan—they began to menace Harold's supremacy. All this was in the late autumn of 1065, the rebellion having surprised Tostig's capital at York in the early part of October. The rebels took the son of Aelfgar, called Morcar, for their Earl in Tostig's place, through him acquired great new levies from Lincoln and Nottingham and Derby, while Morcar's brother Edwin joined in with those of Leicester, and as was always happening when there was civil war, the anti-government party allied itself with the Welsh, and there were Welsh invaders with that army as it went south. That army also did what all rebel armies did in the unfortunate England of the eleventh century, it went raiding about the villages, carrying off hundreds of men into slavery or for ransom, killing and burning.

Harold met them and accepted their terms. It was not merely that he found them a formidable force—he would have fought them, strong as they were, if it had been only that—it was more that he had to have as many people behind him as possible in the plan which he had now certainly made of usurping the throne. For King Edward was not far from death. Harold must be at the capital, he must be at Court, he must be ready to act at once. He was back in London just before the opening of December, and barely three weeks later, on Christmas Eve, Edward had become so ill that his death seemed a matter of hours. He had lived long enough to see the completion of his great new Church at Westminster, the Abbey of St. Peter, which he had so lavishly endowed, but he did not see its consecration, for when that high ceremony took place on Childermas (the 28th of December), he was too ill to move. He survived only for a week, and on the vigil of Twelfth Day, the 5th of January 1066, he died. It is almost certain that on his deathbed, though in what condition of his failing mind we do not know, he commended the care of the kingdom to Harold and may even have appointed him as his successor.

All England felt the blow, and was in dread of what was to come. St. Edward [the Confessor] had endeared himself to the people, his just reputation for great holiness had made of him almost a legendary figure—one might say without disrespect, an idol; the detested Danish tradition of wars, usurpations, massacres and torturings stood in contrast to the plain fact that in spite of so much turmoil and misery continuing in the half-Danish power of Godwin and his sons, there had at least been a native King upon the throne; and that constant tradition of the blood royal of Wessex, going back through five centuries to the half-mythical British King with his British name of Cedric, was a sacred possession. Now it had come to an end and there was no valid heir. The alien exiled Aetheling was dead, the child in his teens who remained was not valid and could not be seriously considered as a candidate.

But whatever popular feeling may have been, Harold gave it no time for expression; he acted with a rapidity that was indecent. He buried his old lord at once, on the Twelfth Day itself, the very morrow of his death, and having about him and under him such of the Council as then were in London, had himself immediately proclaimed King. Such a proclamation, however, meant nothing until he had been crowned, for it was crowning that made a King in those days, and one not yet crowned and anointed had not royal authority over the minds of men. Even while Edward's grave was still open, or freshly covered, on the very day of the funeral and under the same roof where that grave yawned, above and within a very few yards of it, Harold was enthroned, anointed and crowned. He had seized and grasped like a man of battle that he was.

The news of the holy King's death and of the immediate usurpation that followed came almost at the same moment across the sea to William. The issue was joined. Harold was not secure, and he knew it. He held the south, the north was still doubtful. He had even been at the pains to see that the slur of coronation by Stigand, his own Archbishop, should not weaken him further, and he had had the crown put upon his head by the Archbishop of York. But what was rising upon him like a thundercloud was the active effort of his brother Tostig, who had taken refuge with his father-in-law, Baldwin of Flanders, at Bruges and was gathering forces for an attack. Tostig had a fleet of sixty sail in the Belgian waters, he had gone over to see his brother-in-law in the Court of Normandy, of whom to make an ally he had got the promise of help from Hardrada, the King of Norway; and while he still awaited that reinforcement he, after the fashion of his family, harried the south English coasts, only sailing back when Harold's force approached, and biding his time till the Norwegians could come and join him. He sailed up the east coast of England, was beaten off, took refuge with Malcolm, the King of Scotland who had married the Aetheling's sister, St. Edward's niece, and there in the north awaited the coming of the Scandinavians.

Meanwhile William had acted with that ponderance and exact calculation of effect which so strongly supported by restraint the intensity of his temper. He had summoned his council and told them of his determination to enforce his claim; he sent his envoy over to recall to Harold that famous oath of allegiance and his promise of support; to which Harold made answers with every plea at his command. He said that he had sworn under compulsion; and here was ambiguity, for though it was true that the oath had been taken at William's own Court, surrounded by all the strength of the Norman Duchy, yet it had been taken by Harold not only in freedom but after a splendid reception and in the midst of men who had treated him as a comrade in arms. He said that the Crown of England depended upon the English Council, which could be said in a sense to have acted, for he had relied upon such of the Council as were in London and immediately in his power. That was Harold's reply. But whatever the excuses, the essential was that he clearly intended to maintain his usurpation by force of arms, and the odds seemed certainly upon his side—*if* he could maintain himself against the blow that was threatening him from the north of England.

He stood awaiting the threatened invasion from the French coast, he had taken position for it in Sussex, when the expected news of the trouble 200 miles away reached him: the King of Norway had carried out his promise; by August he had gathered a very great fleet of 300 ships, and Tostig, who had lost most of his armament in the early defeated raid upon the east coast, joined him with such few sail as he had gathered in the mouth of the Tyne.

Edwin and Morcar, now Earls of the north by their agreement with Harold, were loyal to that agreement and tried to save York. They failed. The great Norwegian host with Tostig sailed up the Humber to the Ouse, and after a violent fight overcame the Earls at York, and the north with York was surrendered.

Now did the high talent of Harold the soldier appear. Upon hearing of the advent of the Norwegians coming in aid of his rebellious brother, and before the news of their success at York had reached him, he was marching northward with that rapidity which he had always shown, and with troops to whom he must have given unity through his power of command—as is proven by what followed. Thus to march northward and abandon the coast threatened by the Norman invasion was a campaign in which chance seemed to help him—the chance of weather. For violent westerly winds were sweeping the Channel; with the season approaching the equinox the tempests might succeed each other, and William's opportunity be long deferred. But that steadfast enemy behind whom was now the opinion of all Europe, with that of the Papacy which he championed, was tenaciously awaiting his moment, in spite of time and check. All his own lords of Normandy had rallied to him, the prelates and the great feudatories had offered him ships in quantities apart from those which his own large revenue could supply, and which he had been building with astonishing energy all that summer and the spring—ever since the end of the winter. Indeed, the preparations had begun before the winter was over, with February, and now that the autumn had come, all was ready for the stroke. That armament, of a size hitherto quite unknown even in the height of the Scandinavian efforts by sea, he had gathered off the mouth of the Dives in the Bessin, to the west of the mouth of the Seine. Thence he summoned them to meet him further east, up the coast, intending to sail at last from St. Valéry bay. But that same violent northerly storm which had put heart into Harold treated the new Norman fleet hardly, there were many wrecks on the way east against the lee shore before all were gathered in the estuary of the Somme—which is the bay of St. Valéry between that town and the hook of Crotoy—and there lay anchored awaiting a change in the wind. Even so, it was the greatest naval armament that the north had ever seen.

There were of all craft some 3000; even the large transports, which had been special gifts from the great feudatories, amounted themselves alone to no less than 780 large vessels, contributed by fourteen of the great lords—from the Abbot of St. Ouen, who had provided 20 such ships, to Odo, Bishop of Bayeux, and William's half-brother, who sent 100, and the Count of Mortain, who sent 120. Besides these the host of lesser men must have sent great numbers; William himself provided presumably much more than the greatest feudatory, and the large ships had smaller craft attendant upon them. The number of fighting men to be transported was some fifty or sixty thousand, but to these must be added a great number of workers; there were the ships' crews, and the fully mounted knights were (by one tradition) 14,000, therefore at least that number of horses were sent across, and certainly a great many more.

Up in the north of England Harold, by an astonishingly rapid march, had appeared in time with a sufficient force to meet Tostig's rebellion and the great mass of the Norwegians. It was upon the 20th of September, under a north-east gale, that Hardrada and Tostig had got York. Four days later Harold fell upon them, effecting apparently a complete strategic surprise.

The King of Norway had left one large part of his men on board his ships; the others were dispersed, organizing the conquest of Yorkshire. While they were thus occupied and divided, Harold was upon them. Hardrada and Tostig concentrated at top speed and fell back eastward by the Roman road to Stamford Bridge upon the Derwent, a short day's march away, and there Harold's host, in spite of its tremendous march of between two and three hundred miles (many units must have covered at least 250), was pressing them hard. They sent urgently for the forces still on board the Norwegian ships to come up and reinforce them, but before these could arrive the action was joined. The first blows had not been struck when Harold, anxious to be off south and to be rid of this great peril so that he might meet the other still greater one that menaced, offered to give back the Earldom of the north to Tostig. He was told it was too late, for what was to be given to Hardrada? And Harold made the famous answer, "Seven feet of land for a grave"—for Hardrada had the tall Scandinavian stature.

Three hundred ships meant about 15,000 men or possibly less. Harold's host may not have been more numerous than this after so long and sudden a march, but it had only to deal with a part of the Norwegian forces. These therefore stood on the defensive, fighting on foot as the defensive was always ordered to do, and forming a ring with the spearmen all around and a line of spears fixed in the ground pointing outward to receive the first shock. That ring was charged by Harold's cavalry, and the battle took the form of an intense offensive attempting to break the iron of this defense, Hardrada showing his huge form in the midst of the turmoil, with burnished helm and, like Sobieski before Vienna, a fine blue cloak distinguishing him from among them all. The defense might have succeeded and worn out the attack had not the ring been broken by men eager to pursue when the exhausted cavalry at moments retired. Hardrada fell, shot through the neck by an arrow, and Tostig took over command—then the reinforcement from the ships came up, too late, for the unity of the defense was gone. The slaughter was not completed until Tostig himself was dead, and nearly all the leaders who had taken York those few days before.

This was the 27th of September, Wednesday. If the north-westerly gale still blew, it was dying down, for on the very next day, in the Channel, it no longer threatened the project of the Normans. The wind there, though slight enough, was turning southerly, and the days of waiting and of prayers were ended. William and his host went aboard on that day, Thursday, the 28th of September, Michaelmas Eve, as the flood was covering the wide mud-flats of Valéry bay, and the miles of ship-craft, large and small, swung aslant between the westward-making current and the little air from the south. It was near dusk before the slack water came at the height of the tide, and then orders were given to set sail, the Duke's ship leading with a light on the masthead for all to follow, and at the prow the gilded statue of a boy pointing towards the further shore. The new moon at her first quarter lay over the cliffs of Normandy to the west. Duke William's leading ship started almost due north-west, the tide taking him somewhat down channel through the darkness.

They ran at five or six knots. When day broke, they were already near enough to the English shores, east and south of Beachy Head, to be within cable depth for the Duke; for the morning being hazy, and seeing no other craft near him, he dropped anchor to let the rest come up. He sent one up the mast-head who could still see nothing, but a little later the watcher announced as it were a forest of masts arriving through the brume as it lifted. They had broached a cask of wine on the deck, and William was drinking prosperity to his rights. The *Mora* got up her anchor again, and ran for the stump of Pevensey Castle to the north above the shoreline, a Roman thing.

What is now Pevensey level, between Beachy Head and Hastings, was in that time a great land-locked harbor, much as Portsmouth is today, and the way into it was by narrows, the western side of which were guarded by the castle, while the eastern side formed the end of a long spit of shingle and sand, thrown up as these beaches are along the Sussex coast. In the midst of the first flood in mid-morning of that Michaelmas Day the *Mora* ran through the narrows into the wide calm water within, and all the great fleet followed. By three in the afternoon, when it was high-water, the bigger ships had all been beached in line along the landward side of the spit, and the disembarkation of men and horses and provisions and munitions began. Moreover, they cast up a defensive work across the neck of the spit to prevent a surprise attack upon the ships thus drawn up.

They were men of all kinds, from all parts of Gaul and even from Italy, with an undue proportion of territorial men—the small nobles and their free followers—who had come to try their fortunes, to be rewarded with land or place if William should succeed, to be captive or slain, or (most improbably) get back over sea, if he should fail. The great revenues and the economy of the Duke of Normandy had also hired very many of them as mercenaries, for a time. The core of it all was of course from Normandy, both of nobles and of freemen, but there were also many from the southern and central provinces, and a host of Bretons and a host of Flemings—all drawn up in the camp which was pitched on that Michaelmas Day beside Pevensey harbor. William rode off at once with a small band to seize Hastings, a dozen miles up the coast, and its castle, which he garrisoned; and meanwhile Harold's scouts were galloping in relays northward to announce the landing to Harold. Duke William's men, foraging far and wide to add to their provisions, were tied here to the very region of their landing. They dared not move in bulk lest they should leave their transports open to attack and their sole chance of retirement in case of defeat destroyed.

But even as it was, the chance of defeat was small. William must obtain a complete victory, or see the whole of his host almost certainly destroyed—for they could not live for long on what they had or by mere foraging, and the sea was now closely guarded by every ship that Harold could press into the service. These indeed had watched the shores and would have fought the invading fleet had it come earlier, but after those storms which had so much damaged William's own craft on the further shore before he finally sailed, these ships of Harold's had gone round into the Thames to refit, and they had not come back till these few days too late, after the invasion had been accomplished.

Harold's abilities as a commander, already so well proved in Wales, and far more strikingly illustrated by that very rapid march of so large a body to the north and his victory at Stamford Bridge, were now put to the last and greatest test, and he rose to it magnificently. It may have been by the third day, it can hardly have been earlier, that the news reached him, and he set out at once for London. That he could bring with him the whole of his host at such a pace is not conceivable, for that forced march must have been covered in a week. But his personal guard, the house-carles, accomplished it, and, we may suppose, the best disciplined and more compact of his units. But even so, it meant a very long forced march every day. It is difficult to understand how it was accomplished, but we know that it was so, and it is full proof of Harold's powers of command. He must have left orders long before, when first the invasion threatened, for the gathering of forces in the south. He knew what numbers he would need, for he had decided upon the position he would take up and upon which he would fight in Sussex; he was prepared to bring thither, in a further extraordinary march of 70 miles in three days and two nights from the Thames to Battle, his own personal forces, such units as he could concentrate in London, joined, presumably, by levies from south of the river. He also in this amazing swallowing up of distance managed to bring with him his heavy armament, the catapults, which he was to use in his final battle.

There runs, as everybody knows, a great Roman road, most of which is still in use (nearly all of it has recently been put back into use), from Dover through Canterbury to London Bridge. What is less known is that there also ran a Roman road branching off from this last at Rochester to the port of Hastings. All marching in those days, especially when it involved heavy wheeled traffic, was tied to the still used Roman roads, as you may see by the sites of the battles.

The reason that this Roman road ran from Rochester to Hastings was that there was at Hastings still in use from Roman times a secure harbor, defended by that castle which William had seized. This harbor was formed by a projecting ridge of chalk rock, standing out as the Needles do today (though lower) from the shore and curving round towards the castle height. In the succeeding centuries since the Conquest it has slowly been washed away; it had already grown insecure by Elizabethan times; but in 1066 it was of high importance.

Now this Roman road from Rochester to Hastings cuts transversely, about six miles before reaching the sea, a peculiar formation, excellent as a defensive position in that time when a defense would have to be held mainly against heavy armed cavalry. It may be described as having the shape of a hammer, or "T": along the handle of the hammer runs the road on a ridge, the cross-piece forms another ridge, steep towards the south, very steep at either end, sloping off more easily at the back towards the north. This cross-piece, or ridge, with its steep approach from the front and its easily defended flanks, where the ground falls so sharply at either end, is somewhat less than a mile long, just over 1600 yards. It would need, to defend it against great masses of heavy cavalry deployed and charging up that slope—steep though the slope was—certainly more than 20,000 men and more probably 30,000 if, as was the case in this battle, the opponents were more numerous still. You must allow for files at least twelve deep, and better twenty; twelve, or better twenty, ranks one behind the other along the ridge from flank to flank. This was the position which Harold reached with all his men on the evening of Friday, October the 13th, the eve of St. Calixtus. We do not know the name of that ridge, on which there then seems to have been no village. It certainly could not have been called Senlac, though this strange southern French form is attached to it by one writer a lifetime afterwards.

William, lying in Hastings, with his great host encamped about him six miles away, had ample warning of the approach. On the morning of the morrow, Saturday, St. Calixtus's Day, the 14th of October, he heard Mass very early, communicated, and sent out his orders for the advance in the last hours of the darkness. By eight o'clock at latest his host had arrived and was deploying before the summits of the slope called Telham, which faces from the south the ridge upon which Harold's line was drawn up. The Normans were in the center, on either side of the Roman road, the Flemings to the right or east, facing that end of the ridge opposite, which lies above the point where the railway station is now; the Bretons on the left or west, mainly it may be presumed on foot, for they had between them and the western end of the ridge above them, marshy fields to cross with a brook running through: an obstacle which made advance more and more difficult as one went further to the west down the line of it.

At about nine o'clock William's force, all deployed, was set in motion down the slope towards the valley, and on the ridge beyond stood that immovable line, all on foot as the defensive demanded (the horses left behind, as was the universal rule on the defensive), ready to engage in battle when the shock should come and to discharge from the catapults their missiles against the feudal cavalry. There is a fine story, handed down from a generation later, telling how in front of the very center of the Norman line slowly rode the minstrel Taillefer, tossing his sword in the air like a juggler and catching it by the hilt again, and singing as he went the song of Roland and the Peers who died at Roncesvalles.

The strongest formation in the line, nearly a mile long, which was now advancing down Telham hill, was of course the center. Its own strongest element again were the heavy-armed knights, most of them presumably the direct feudal tenants of the Duke. They were also presumably all of them—as were the armed gentry and more considerable freemen of the auxiliaries, Flemings, Bretons, and men from the south and center of Gaul—covered by the long coat of mail which completely protected the body to below the knees, a mass of steel rings interlocked on to themselves and on to the leather foundation, or perhaps sometimes an independent network of steel rings, pulled on over the unarmored garment beneath. On the head they wore the conical metal helmet, not completely covering it, as yet, even in the case of the wealthy, with a vizor, but continuing in a broad nosepiece which partially defended the face and already, in this early development of the helmet, made it difficult to recognize the wearer. On the left arm they wore a long oval shield rounded at the top and pointed at the lower end; slung from a band on the left of the body was a leather sheath with its sword, and borne in the right hand, which was free of the reins, the lance, which was the principal weapon used in the charge.

In front of these bodies of horsemen went a line of archers. This was an arm which had been rapidly improved and developed beyond the Channel during the past twenty years; the bow was short, the trajectory of the arrow not flat as it became later with the long bow, so that the missile was apparently of most service when the archers aimed high, when the arrow fell perpendicularly at the end of its flight of maximum range, shooting down by the weight of its iron tip.

On either side and perhaps also interspersed with the mounted men were the mass of the lesser fighters; these were on foot, as the archers were, but not fully trained as was that comparatively small body. Such levies were hastily summoned, and even when they were, as many of them were, mercenaries, they were under poor control and hired themselves only for short periods, fighting not only for gain but for loot. What proportion this ill-organized part of the fifty or sixty thousand bore to the heavily armed gentry and men-at-arms we do not know; but it is fairly safe to say that there were not less than 14,000 horse, and there may have been more.

The long line crossed the lowest level of the shallow valley—they were already perhaps molested by the stones from Harold's catapults—till they stood at the foot of the short but steep slope beyond. Along the ridge of that slope they saw before them nearly a mile of men in dense packed lines, one line behind the other; there was no stockade, unless there may have been some rapidly improvised pointed pickets to check the cavalry charge. Their defenses were the tall men of England—the superior height of the islanders, and indeed of nearly all the northern races, over the French was remarked throughout Europe; it was a cause of jest for instance to the Germans in the Italian struggle, an insult which brought German prisoners upon one occasion to torture.

The action opened with a discharge of arrows, the object of which was to shake the defense by the fall of missiles on a high trajectory throughout all parts of the very dense defending line. That line seems, save for the catapults, to have had no missile weapons; it depended mainly, at least for the most heavily armed, upon the Danish battle-axe: but we must remember that a great portion of Harold's command—probably the majority of it—was armed hastily and imperfectly and variously, not sufficiently. For many of them must have come up hurriedly, summoned from the southern shires and from London. Harold's own position of command was of course in the center, in front of which the approach to the ridge was steepest; he there stood with his two brothers, having set up his standard of the Fighting Man worked upon cloth with gold thread. We know the spot; it is immediately to the east of the present ruins, somewhat behind them, where now still appear, just showing above ground, the foundations of what was later the High Altar of the Abbey. The original slope up to the ridge at this, its central part, is now not to be determined, as it has been replaced by a wall and terrace; but it seems to have been about one in five at the steepest part; on the two flanks, to the left and right of the center, it is very much less, one in ten, one in fifteen, and in places even flatter.

After this first discharge of arrows the archers fell back and the heavy cavalry charged. The charge failed. The horses were turned back again down the hill to renew the effort. But in the first part of the action, at what precise moment we do not know, but perhaps before noon, came an incident which was characteristic. We have seen its fellow determining the victory for Harold at Stamford Bridge, and it was here to determine the victory for William. It lay in [the] lack of discipline inevitably present in all feudal bodies. There was on this ridge of battle a knoll, still conspicuous though now masked with trees, standing out somewhat in front of the crest of the low ridge on the west of the line, opposite the Bretons. The Bretons here swarming up the slope broke, and the defenders at that spot began to abandon their strict formation and to pursue. The opportunity was immediately seized by William: the nearest heavy cavalry, the armed mounted gentry from the center, swept in behind the isolated rash body which had thus detached itself from the height of the knoll; it was surrounded and completely destroyed.

It became later an established story upon the Norman side that the incident gave William the idea of a ruse; he would affect these same occasional flights, and, when he had thus tempted portions of Harold's line to abandon formation and venture themselves down the slope in pursuit again, surround such isolated bodies and wipe them out. We may doubt the story of the ruse. It is hardly consonant with the mixed turmoil of continuous fighting which went on hour after hour all that October day. It is more probable that this frequent breaking of ranks on the side of the defense was spontaneous, and followed upon successive checks suffered by the charges, as each was repelled. At any rate, whether designed or not, each cutting off of isolated rash advances lessened the numbers, and weakened the solidity, of the defense. Yet Harold's line as a whole was so packed and strong that it still stood firm and seemed unbreakable, even by that vast weight of horse, men and metal which broke upon it in successive waves. The battle-axe had proved superior to the lance and the sword, and the men on foot, as long as they stood in formation, a match for the Norman cavalry, for horses always swerve at the point of contact with a steadfast infantry.

The exhaustion suffered by the opposing thousands was greater upon the side of the attack than of the defense, it was the attack which had to cover far the most ground, repeatedly advancing, thrown back and then readvancing, while the most of the defensive stood unmoved. The French had to make the effort of breasting repeatedly the slope against men who stood secure upon the level summit. The strain and confusion was such that in the latter part of the action, perhaps in the mid afternoon and not long before the close, the cry ran along the line of the invaders that William himself had fallen, and there seems to have been some short period of lull during which the cohesion of the offensive was in peril. It might have broken and decided the day. For if after so awful an effort of so many hours without food, and suffering the heaviest losses, the Norman, Breton and Flemish line had given way, all was certainly lost. There would have been fierce pursuit through the last hour of daylight and the dark; the sea was blockaded by Harold's ships, few—perhaps none—of the remnants would have returned. Not only the great invading force, but William's own power and the unity of the Duchy which he had raised to such a pitch of power before the expedition, would have dissolved. In that lull the Duke by his personal action rallied the line. Horses had been killed under him; he rode on a fresh mount up and down before them, having lifted his helm from his head so that his face could be seen, and so inspired the final and desperate effort which was to be made.

Once again the broad wave of men and horses took the slope with what was left to them of energy and fury. The day was already declining; it was between half-past four and five o'clock, and the struggle had taken the form of a close mêlée all along the line of the top of the ridge under the slanting rays of the late autumn sun, now near its setting. The defensive still stood, but a last discharge of arrows may have shaken it. Harold's brother had already fallen; he himself was still alive and in command, standing by his banner, when one of the arrows falling from over the front line struck him in the eye and pierced the brain, and he fell.

Even as when it was believed that William had fallen a little while earlier, and as that rumor had so nearly decided the great issue against the Duke, so now in that "last quarter of an hour" with Harold's fall the thing was done. Of the opposing lines, by this time wholly intermingled, it was the defensive that broke. The Flemish and Breton foot upon either flank swarmed over the level of the ridge, and the heavy cavalry broke right through the center as the sun set. Twenty Norman knights fought their way through the still resisting clot at the center to Harold's banner, for the honor of his capture; and one of them, to the lasting anger of William, struck at the dead body with his sword.

But this was only an episode in the now complete defeat of the great soldier who had fallen. As the darkness gathered, the survivors of the defensive were in full flight back into the wood-lands of the Weald beyond the ridge, or to their horses on the Roman road: the pursuit was fierce, the losses of the chaos into which Harold's flying command was reduced were heavy, out of all proportion to what they had suffered while their line still stood. Such of them as were saved were saved by the night, and one considerable body by an accident of ground upon the right center. There was here behind the ridge on the further slope of it a very deep trench which can still be traced and which the Normans in their traditions of the battle called "the evil hollow." Into this, it being now almost dark, the mounted leaders of the pursuit stumbled; and the Count of Boulogne, William's nephew among them, was beaten back with the blood streaming from his nose and face. William in person rallied that check again—it was the last isolated episode of the victory and disaster. After it came the night: half relieved in its final hours by the old moon in her last quarter, rising over Rother to the east. William had his tent set upon the spot where his enemy had fallen, and there supped, in the midst of the dying and the dead. As for Harold, the victor ordered his body to be taken south and buried on the sands of the seashore, for a symbol. But later it was redeemed, and put to rest with royal honors before the altar of Waltham, which he had founded, the Norman nobles attending.

Ordeal by battle had been tried and the decision given. It remained to reap the fruits of victory. Even in the first days of that task the difficulty which William had not suspected or not allowed for appeared—the interference with his plans that must follow from the composition of his great army. One quarter of it had fallen on that field of Hastings. By so much was it reduced. But the survivors saw before them above all an opportunity for spoil, while William's object was to enter peacefully upon the power which was rightly his—as he so sincerely thought; and which the judgment of God himself—as he also firmly believed—had given him: right confirmed in action. He would enter peacefully into the administration of this great new realm as he had entered into the lesser but considerable addition of Maine. He would rule contented subjects by their own customs—indeed in those days it would be impossible to rule otherwise, for custom was everything. He would be the King of England as he had been for so long the increasingly powerful Duke of Normandy and Count of Maine, strongly organizing a people at peace.

But the instrument upon which alone he could rely upset all those plans. Petty loot and spoil for the lesser men, rewards in land for their leaders, increase of wealth for all—this was what appeared the immediate advantage to be gained by those thousands, who had followed him, as all feudal levies did, for their own increase, and who were, as all feudal levies were, ill coordinated: at the best preserving some order by units under great lords, at the worst small bodies out for plunder, and, what is more, feeling their own peril in the midst of men whom they know not and of an alien speech. It was not an army in the modern sense which William thus commanded overseas, cut off from their own land; it was such a loose body of individuals or lesser units, bound only for short service, and if that service were to be prolonged, expecting as a matter of right a corresponding reward.

I have said that the first signs of this difficulty that was to meet him appeared at once. It was when, after the battle, William rode to Dover to occupy that town and harbor and castle and thus further secure his communications. The castle accepted his garrison without resistance, but the common soldiers maltreated the townsmen, looted, set fire to houses. The Duke paid compensation for these losses, but it was an omen of what was to come. Still tenacious and not to be moved from his first plan, he went on to the next step: he must be crowned; for until he was crowned and anointed, he was not King. The obstacle was London, wherein, or rather just outside the walls thereof, he would thus set the first seal upon his new power. But London was too great to be taken at a blow; it was the largest city of northern Christendom, far larger than any with which William had had to deal at home, more than a mile square of walled and defended town with a broad tidal estuary between the south and it—a mass of wealth and stores.

The strategy William pursued was well thought out. He marched westward with his diminished force, diminishing it still further by the garrisons he had to leave at each point where road or bridge from the south ran towards the city. He thus curved round, through Kent and Surrey and Berkshire, nor made any effort to cross the Thames till he came to Wallingford, four days' march to the west of the capital which he had thus already in part isolated. As he passed to the south of London on this way, he had been attacked by some organized force sent out against him to the southern bank of the river; he had easily repelled it. At Wallingford the local official in command of all the district at once admitted his rule, and hither came also the man who most trembled for the result that would follow to himself from this ordeal by battle—Stigand, the center of offense—completely submitting himself. The English Council was divided. The laymen seem to have been for attempting a further resistance, the lands and revenues of these great lords were at stake; but no one had come to it from the north, the south and west were cut off, and in such a maimed assembly, uncertain how to act, the Church stood for William and for the end of that anarchy which had torn England ever since the pirates had first begun to harry the land. This minority of a minority of the Council hastily chose the boy Edgar, the Aetheling's son, to be successor. He was neither by character nor by age fitted for the position, and we have seen how Harold had contemptuously passed him by, with none protesting. But the memory of his uncle, the holy King, and the powerful tradition of the blood royal of Wessex led this portion of the remnant of the Council to their decision. It was quite ephemeral. They surrendered upon William's appearance on the Roman road which comes down from the north to the city, and thenceforward he was, save for his crowning, the admitted King. He had wholly encircled London, save that the town was open, of course, for provision and for commerce by water. Even so, he waited, lying with most of his depleted forces and his nobles to the east, in Essex, until he could make sure of his crowning.

He judged at last, in December, that the moment had come, and passing through the city with his host he was solemnly crowned at Westminster upon Christmas Day, the eleventh week after the battle of Hastings, and was at last King indeed, with moral right by all the mind and custom of the time to obedience from all the realm that had obeyed his cousin Edward. But even in such a day the obstacle he could not overcome appeared—the turbulence and lack of order in his men.

The traditional story goes that the Norman soldiery on guard outside the Abbey thought the King was being attacked within the building when they heard the shouts of acclamation which were part of the customary ritual at a coronation, and that, fearing an insurrection, they began to burn the neighboring houses. It is an improbable explanation. It is much more likely either that there were quarrels between these soldiers and the inhabitants, or that they took the opportunity for loot. If not, why did not they go into the church to save William, instead of despoiling the houses around?

The Duke was increasingly anxious as the danger of the situation became clearer to him. In that Continental warfare of which alone he had experience, the feudal force levied for a very short service of a few weeks could be disbanded without peril at the end of it, if its task had been accomplished. Moreover, it had commonly fought within, or close to, the country to which its members belonged. But here it was impossible to dismiss the army after those first few weeks; he had to depend upon it month after month and year after year for at least four years, until, after a great deal more trouble, pacification was achieved. Further, it was necessary to build castles, some of them substantial fortresses of stone, others (the greater part, no doubt) no more as yet than stockades or mounds, but everywhere the business demanded time. He needed such protection for his garrisons, and a garrison he must have in all the principal towns as well as the points which were of military importance—where the main roads crossed the rivers, for instance; or where there was a junction of several ways. He obtained the continuance of the army, as to the mercenary part of it by renewed payments, as to the part which depended upon allegiance by grants of land; but here it is important to understand what the distribution of land seems to have been which followed upon the victory of Hastings.

There was no very general confiscation. It would have been impossible in any case to carry out, and the attempt to do so would have rendered William's difficulties tenfold greater. What there was was principally a change in the great heads of the system, the magnates, between the Crown and the lesser men. All the personal lordships of Godwin's house went, of course, direct to the new dynasty; but when we read of such and such of William's great nobles (his half-brother Odo, for instance), that he was given such and such a number of manors, we must understand it to mean overlordship quite as often as true possession.

The chief economic effect of the change was the stricter and more burdensome levy of funds for the head of the State. The old administration under a very few earls, constantly quarreling among themselves, almost independent, had been oppressive enough—but not oppressive through strict organization. William introduced the beginnings of a modern fisc [state treasury]. He took advantage of the Danegeld, with its general assessment of 2s. to the hide (roughly today somewhere over 6d. to the arable acre, but less than 1s.). What perhaps was more severely felt, he came to gather it with great regularity and under an organization such as the older and slacker state of affairs had not known. Also, what today we might call the new registration of land, the confirmation of title, was oppressive. Men who had supported Harold were naturally regarded as having lost their land; they could often (perhaps nearly always) recover it, but they would have to pay the full dues, much as a man would do upon the death of one from whom he inherited the manorial rights. And there was also inevitably a considerable measure of confiscation, especially in the case of those who had actually fought against William.

The difficulties which now began to arise in his settlement of England were not due to confiscation, still less were they due to what, by a complete misreading of history, some of our moderns, especially in the last century, have put down to what is today national feeling. Feudal society knew nothing of such a feeling except in its vaguest form; what it did understand and felt strongly was allegiance to a lord; but it did not need national feeling to create friction between a mass of armed men scattered among a far more numerous population which spoke a different tongue, and those armed men under a loose discipline which, where their local chief was himself inclined to pillage, was melted into no discipline at all. In London, where William felt the chief danger might arise, he took every precaution; he withdrew from it again to its neighborhood, to the east, at Barking, where his Court was filled with the English nobility, large and small. There they did him homage and there he began the confirmation of the new titles to land. And among them, treated with especial honor, was the Aetheling, Edgar. After the first six months William believed, and for the moment it seemed true, that his task was achieved; and taking with him a number of English, including those higher men who were as much hostages as guests (Stigand and Edwin, the Earl of Mercia; and Morcar, the Earl of Northumbria, and the Earl of Huntingdon and Northampton, Waltheof), he went back in March 1067 to show himself in Normandy and to strengthen his position by a triumph. It is curious to note that the magnificence of the English wealthier class particularly struck the people of Normandy—the expense of their clothing, the silk materials and ornaments in the precious metals, and their possession of foreign stuffs and goods which a trade, especially that of the great port of London, permitted them.

But in William's absence there arose a great deal of disorder, and it grew worse the longer he stayed away. Odo, who had the government of Kent and therefore the main communications with Europe and the approaches to London, was oppressive and unwise. The rest of the country, however, under Fitz Osbern, was even more disturbed than the southeast. How little all this sort of thing was national one can see by the action of the men of Kent, who in their abortive rebellion were supported by Eustace of Boulogne, the man who had married Edward the

Confessor's sister and who had fought on William's side at Hastings. In the north, which had a standing tradition of rebellion against the regular government, there was especial violence. And already during the first days of his presence in Normandy the Duke had heard of the faithful native lord whom he had set over Northumbria being murdered. He set yet another native over the north, but he never knew when he might not be threatened with the loss of all that further territory which he had never visited.

By the December of 1067 he was constrained to return, and it was high time, for the next year (1068) was a series of sporadic outbreaks, the most serious being that of Exeter—a confused movement, the motives of which are obscure but probably connected with the new taxes. Therein lay Githa, Harold's mother, hitherto undisturbed, but after this to be an exile. William settled the Exeter trouble without difficulty, and characteristically, for the moment without cruelty, and with the use of native troops; he was still intent upon doing all he could not to exasperate, but to pacify. This policy of engaging English mercenaries in increasing numbers to supply the place of the foreigners, who presumably had begun to be sent back overseas, was all part of the same scheme, and he got willing service enough. But the north still remained like a thundercloud, standing (as it had always stood, or rather its leaders) for the chance of greater wealth through independence of the taxing power on the Thames.

By way of example and terror he ravaged it fearfully, kept his Christmas in York itself, and made his famous march rather more than two months later in despite of storms and snow through the Pennines, under the grumblings of mutiny, and seized Chester; and with that, by this year of 1070, one may say that his realm was at last secured. But it had been at the expense of his abandoning, under the compulsion of the increasing strain, his original policy of mildness and acceptation by consent.

Henceforward more and more do we find men of William's own speech and culture put into the chief places, and especially, as vacancies occurred, into the chief places of the Church. That they should have the chief military places was necessary, but that he should so act with the bishoprics was indeed a symptom that his first policy could no longer be continued. And the first sign of this was the filling of the great diocese of Dorchester (running right across England from north to south), after the death of the old Bishop who had held it under King Edward, by Remigius (Remy) of Fécamp.

There remained one isolated center of disturbance. It was a distant, ill-frequented spot on the edge of the Fens not far from Cambridge, the slight lump of rising land known as Ely, on which had long stood a monastery. The trouble there was even more confused in motive than the other sporadic anarchies had been. It grew to be nothing more definite than a center to which anyone might rally who hoped for something to come to him out of the breakdown of order. At the head of the little settlement was a certain Hereward—the whole thing was so picturesque, especially in its conclusion, that a mass of legend arose round it, songs and myths, so that it is very difficult to disentangle the facts. There is no doubt that Hereward was of a courageous, unscrupulous sort which always makes brigands or rebels; he may have been the son of a family which had lost its land in the confiscations, he was almost certainly a relative of the last Abbot of Peterborough.

When, on the Abbacy falling vacant in 1069, William appointed a new Abbot of the new sort, Turold, to bring in the more vigorous organization of the Continent, Hereward sallied out from his refuge and attacked him on his way. He was joined by a remaining group of pirates, and between them they burnt the Abbey, massacred the monks and looted all they could loot. As the outlaws remained unpunished in their isolated "island"—it was really something of an island, with great marshes and flats of water round it, as it would be today if the great drainage system of the Fens were to break down—they were joined by others, men who came from any number of differing personal motives, but each with a grievance and each with the obscure feeling that making it difficult for the new state of affairs might help to restore some of the advantages he had had under the old. Great men took refuge there, the Bishop of Durham, and Edwin and Morcar, and at last—a great deal too late—William moved. He had hoped perhaps that the thing was so sporadic and local that it would die down or could be dealt with by some feudal superior close at hand; but it had lasted too long and had become too important. The King therefore undertook in person and with large forces the reduction of the island of Ely. He watched all the avenues through which escape might be made by water, and had ships guarding the Wash against any effort of the besieged to escape down river to the sea. There was no chance of taking the place (for the small number of people on it could be long provisioned from the large stores they had) save by regular works. These were undertaken with William's customary skill, energy and tenacity. A causeway was pushed forward through the marsh towards the island, its advancing head and the workmen thereon constantly attacked but the whole going steadily forward, and when it was seen that the inevitable end was at hand the island surrendered.

Even so late and even after his experiences in the north, William maintained what was for his time clemency. As in Maine he mutilated—though he would not kill—the lesser prisoners, the great ones he spared. Edwin had been killed in an earlier attempted flight; Morcar suffered nothing worse than imprisonment. Hereward managed to get away; but it is fairly certain that in good time, when he returned, William received him, was reconciled with him and gave him endowment. The whole thing was over by 1074, and it is from that moment that we can best turn to consider the effect of all this on Europe and the west.

It was undoubtedly greater already than William had envisaged, and it was to produce fruits far greater still. There is a sort of distant parallel between this occupation of England from the south through the energies of William of Falaise and the entry of Gaul into the Graeco-Roman world through the energies of Julius [Caesar]. All this business from Hastings onwards is essentially the re-entry of Britain more fully and finally into the European unity of which of course it had always formed a part; and this showed itself in the ecclesiastical structure of the island, in the economic and political organization of it, in the unity which it founded based on one class of similar habits and speech—to be predominant in a hundred years from the Grampians to the Levant.

It was the Church which had been the principal support of William from the beginning. That universal society with its chief at Rome could not deny the moral system for which it stood and the general acceptance throughout Christendom of William's claim. And William, both by his support and by his reformation and strengthening of the clerical organization, became still more firmly its ally.

Thus, a very necessary piece of reform, part and parcel of the time, recently undertaken in Normandy itself, was here introduced: the separation of the ecclesiastical from the civil courts. It would have come anyhow, for it was spreading all over Europe, but it was specifically William's work. In Normandy, at Rouen for instance, the Archbishop had sat in the same assembly with the Count, and though no doubt when justice was dispensed clerical cases would be dealt with by the Archbishop alone, the lay authority and the ecclesiastical one were parts of a single mixed body. It was inevitable, with the Cluniac spirit now triumphant and the renewal and revivification of the whole Church which it implied, that a separate ecclesiastical court should arise, not only in Normandy but in England.

It will seem strange to many modern readers, but less to those who appreciate what English piety was, that the newcomers were somewhat shocked by, even when they admired, the intense devotion of the island. For instance, unlike the Continent and quite unlike Normandy, England had set up as a regular feast with its appropriate rites the recognition of the Immaculate Conception of Our Lady. The Norman ecclesiastics would not accept that doctrine, or at least not its official pronouncement, and the feast was suppressed save in one or two centers where, notably at Romsey, a local ecclesiastical magnate who had served William well could plead successfully for its continuance.

What much better suited the Norman temper in religion was the equally strong devotion of the English to the traditional doctrine of the Real Presence, in contrast with the recent heresies which had arisen against it. Lanfranc, it will be remembered, had come forward abroad as the chief champion of the Sacrament, and to find the native Church in England devoted to the full dogma was excellent in his eyes. Indeed, England had always been singularly free from heresy. She had received no degrading influence from the Mohammedan pressure so powerful elsewhere: we hear nothing in England of the iconoclastic trouble, for instance, though it might easily have disturbed the first fervid days of the Roman missionaries who re-evangelized the island in the seventh and eighth centuries.

Nowhere do we get the English devotion to the Real Presence more vividly put, even (if I may use the term) more crudely, than in the famous Homilies of Aelfric.

The foundation and chief mark of this reorganization of the religion of England under William was the bringing of Lanfranc to Canterbury. Lanfranc's personality was such that his mere presence was in itself a creative change. Stigand was deposed, his disgraceful pluralities taken from him, but he himself not harshly treated. He could not come and go at will, but his confinement in the castle of Winchester was mild, he was preserved in all his private possessions and had full liberty within its precincts, though at his death his property fell to the Crown.

Upon the 29th of August, 1070, Lanfranc, now an old but still most vigorous man and among the very first figures in Europe, was consecrated Archbishop of Canterbury. He had already refused the Archbishopric of Rouen, presumably because William had thus designed to put him at the head of the Church in England. Further similar appointments followed, and by the time of William's death seventeen years later there was only one native-born Bishop presiding over a diocese in England. Every vacancy as it occurred was filled by William's men.

It proved easier than might have been expected to carry out a policy which strengthened the island and continued to distinguish England by a civil unity hardly to be found in any other province of Christendom. In Normandy itself men had remarked how the Ducal house stood as it were alone, for nearly every great noble was descended from or connected with it, and there were no prominent intermediaries between the central power and the mass of small manorial lords. So it was to be in England, and later the great meeting near Old Sarum (at which not of course all the lords of land [met], as a romantic tradition would have it, but a great and representative concourse of them) affirmed the principle of allegiance paid *direct,* not through intermediate lords but to the King himself. The old policy which had so nearly broken up the island—the division into warring Earldoms—was at an end.

In the matter of economic and social organization William introduced nothing new. Indeed, the world of the twelfth century being what it was, no serious innovations were conceivable. Christendom, especially western Christendom, was one thing; its feudal conceptions everywhere the same, its religion one religion common to all not only in doctrine but in the machinery of Church government; its unity under Rome, its possession of monastic institutions were everywhere under the same rules and leading the same life.

We must here repeat that fundamental truth upon the England of 1074—that there had been no conquest in the modern sense. William was not called a "Conqueror" in the later meaning of the Conquistadores, for instance, who occupied and took over heathen land in America. A conqueror then meant one who had been blessed in his ordeal by battle, who had made good by force his rightful claim, and that was the only conception that the word conveyed to William's mind, or indeed to the mass of his contemporaries. Nor was there "the giving of alien laws." All society was governed everywhere by its customs, each manor living a nearly self-sufficient life, having all its domestic arrangements based on custom, which was sacred. The lord could demand no more than the customary work; the customary tenures, boundaries, privileges, rites and dues were immutable. But what the new administration and the new dynasty could do, and did, was to make precise what had before been vague, to put upon record what had hitherto been traditional, to organize, and to vivify.

Now the most memorable as well as the most salient example of what William of Falaise effected in this manner during his awakening of England was the great survey he ordered, the incomplete but detailed and voluminous record of which later became called "Domesday Book."

This inquiry had two objects: first, William, acting after the logical and precise fashion which is the strength of the Gallic temper as a whole but particularly of the Normans, desired to know exactly where he stood in the matter of revenue. He knew the terms on which he had granted the new tenures to his chief followers, who in their turn received feudal dues from the lesser lords, much the greater part of whom were the original territorial families of the island; but he wanted also to know how the whole economic structure stood insofar as it concerned the manorial system. He had, of course, before him the accounts of those very large stretches of land which had descended from the Imperial Treasury of Rome and were outside the feudal hierarchy of tenure and therefore called "forests"—a term which means "land outside": not only woodlands, but the mountains and great heaths, the waste spaces, and, what is more important, the portions of cultivatable and inhabited land contained within these districts. He knew, or could soon estimate, what revenue would come to him under the term "judgments," that is, fines and confiscations following upon condemnations of individuals in his courts of law. He could make an estimate of what sums would be paid into the royal treasury during the vacancies of bishoprics. But he wanted to know what the whole manorial system was producing for the privileged class of lords, ecclesiastical and lay, whose revenue came from the surplus values formed by the dues which the peasants and burgesses of the towns paid. Only when he knew that could he estimate the economic position of his own greater tenants, as well as the towns and villages of which he was himself direct lord. Only when he knew this could he have an exact account of the sums due to himself from those, large and small, who held directly of the Crown, and of their ability to pay from the dues *they* received from those below them.

This "Domesday" record is something unique in Europe. It

has been of peculiar advantage to English historians, giving them a mass of detail on a very early period of social history such as is not to be found, cataloged and digested, in any other contemporary record of the west. But it also presents a great temptation to that diseased modern appetite which history has caught from the physical scientists, the substitution of hypothesis for proved fact: and it has led to bad errors from the misapprehension of both its motives and its terms.

In the analysis of "Domesday" by modern writers and their orgy of speculation upon the meaning of words which either no one now can understand at all or which can only be guessed at, false conclusions have been drawn which have badly affected our social history. The one thing we do get from "Domesday," within a considerable margin of error, is the total of arable land present at the time of the survey, which was not completed until shortly before the Conqueror's death twenty years after the battle of Hastings.

We know from "Domesday" that the acreage of arable land within the modern boundaries of England (excluding Wales) must have been much what it continued to be throughout the succeeding centuries. This indeed is what anyone might imagine to be the case, for the methods of agriculture and the extent of forest and waste and woodland and fen and the rest were not very materially changed between the eleventh and the seventeenth centuries.

When the pressure of population began in the eighteenth century, and, with it, improved methods of agriculture, there was certainly a greater yield; and by the nineteenth century there was some appreciable increase in the actual area under the plough: but a rough total of some ten million acres within a margin of ten percent may be affirmed, when we have duly estimated for the districts counted in with modern England but not appearing in the "Domesday" survey, and for the arable lands within the forest districts which could not, of their nature, be mentioned in a survey of manorial land.

Now the extreme importance of knowing the arable acreage of any district in the early Middle Ages is that it is the foundation of our estimate upon population. The methods of agriculture were much the same throughout the Middle Ages and on into the seventeenth century; the arable area of a country when it is known not only furnishes us with a foundation for an estimate of its population in agricultural times but some estimate of total wealth as well, though this was increased of course by the craftsmen of the towns and even in the villages, and by the trade of the ports. On such a basis we can confidently say that the population of William's England was more than four million and less than six million souls.

The absurd under-estimate of about two million (or less!) which is solemnly registered in our official textbooks is neither compatible with everything else that we know England to have been in those days nor with the amount of food that must have been produced from the land. We can hardly imagine that such food was produced in order to be thrown away! The false estimate has been got at by counting the number of "Villeins" and others appearing in the survey. But those who so went to work forgot that the "Villeins" and others so mentioned were not human beings, but economic units: when you hear of so many "Villeins," so many "Borderers," and the rest on a particular manor, you are not reading a census of population, but a catalogue of units paying dues. I have used elsewhere a metaphor to explain this error, where I have said that it is as though some historian of the future, hundreds of years hence, were to take the list of the railway stations in Bradshaw and treat it as a complete gazetteer of Great Britain, under the impression that every village had been mentioned in the list of stations.

Undoubtedly what struck contemporaries most about the great survey was its thoroughness. There was an organizing and administrative "drive" behind the new government which was in contrast with the slower society of the last reigns. We can understand also from this survey what is indeed apparent from the map alone—the fact that William, as a consequence of Hastings and his subsequent difficult pacification of the whole realm, had become a much greater personage in Europe even than he had been when he set out to make good his claim. It was not only that he was now possessed of yet another great monarchy, and this one free from any feudal superior whatsoever, but that the scale of the new realm was quite other from the scale of his Continental feudal possessions. Normandy and Maine together, though they formed one of the largest of the provinces, reckoned in arable land—much larger than Flanders, larger than the demesne of the King of France, larger than Brittany or Anjou—are still less than half the new wealth, population and arable land of England. The basis of William's revenue, his recruiting field, and all the rest that made up the strength of a medieval Prince had, by 1074, been multiplied by three, now that he was King of England as well as Duke of Normandy and Count of Maine.

In this began what was later to be so greatly expanded, when his granddaughter's son, the Plantagenet, inherited the realm of England—that novel appearance in the west of a great group of lordships in one realm, all held in one single hand and more than rivalling even the nominal extent of government in the hands of the King of France. From thence therefore came that struggle between the King of France and the King of England—the two chiefs of the French-speaking chivalry of the Middle Ages—as to which should be ultimately the supreme lord of the west. Neither of these rivals succeeded. The King of France, after generations of effort, did unite under himself and control what had been the Continental Plantagenet land; but Plantagenet England escaped him, and from Plantagenet England the claim could be made once more, was nearly established by Edward III, and by alliance and marriage theoretically established by Henry V. The last echoes of this effort at a united western monarchy do not die out until the sixteenth century, when Henry VIII still entertained in a shadowy way the project of re-establishing the connection between his Crown and Gascony.

For, apart from the great feudal expansion of this new dynasty founded by William, which was soon to become by inheritance the Plantagenet dynasty, apart from the regal and feudal conception, there was a social reality now founded, with unity of class between the French-speaking nobles, great and small, on both sides of the Channel, who are to be found within a hundred years permeating Europe, conquering the Holy Land, ruling in Sicily and South Italy, venturing themselves in the reconquest of Spain and established in this island everywhere, save in the Welsh mountains to the west and the Scottish highlands.

* * *

In the last phase of human life there is, for the most of men, and for nearly all active men, a period of some years introductory to death: which years are years of disappointment at the least, and at the most of tragedy. There is on this truth a foreign proverb made for another climate than ours: "Clouds gather at evening." The reasons that this should be so are plain enough. Not only does there come upon all men the realization that from whatever they have known they must be parted, and that all they have called their own being must cease [on this earth]—an active realization which comes commonly late in life—not only, I say, do these things accompany the end of life with all men, but with those who have done much there is an added burden, which is that they must cease from battle; for the body is no longer supporting the immortal mind. And what is more, the petty value of things mortal grows more clearly apparent.

So it was with William of Falaise through those last dozen years he still had to live, his forty-eighth to his sixtieth year. The dates may seem early to be reckoned in a human life as the final dates thereof, but they were the closing of life in this great man. There is a foolish modern custom of saying that our forefathers had shorter lives than ours—the saying is based on that vanity which leisure and loss of faith between them have bred. It is founded also on a false, mechanical, method of judgment. A man having reached maturity had much the same expectation of life in the eleventh as in the twentieth century, save for the accidents of pestilence; the bodies of eleventh-century men were certainly as strong as, or stronger than, those of their descendants. Where men could profit by peace and shelter (as in the clerical profession, which was exempt from arms), very long lives were common enough.

Lanfranc himself, twenty years older than William, survived him by two years. But the class that lived in the saddle, rode at arms or in the chase in all weathers, traveled continuously over the roads of the realm or in foreign expedition, pilgrimage, or raid, the noble class that was exposed to every fatigue and to every risk—*that* class indeed, the class of the great feudatories and of all the territorial lords, had shorter lives than ours. It is difficult today to remember that of old the class which governed was also that which lived under the greatest strain of public service, put itself perpetually in the greatest peril, and suffered beyond others the strain of the body.

William had come now, in the latter seventies of the century—a man approaching the turn of his fiftieth year—to the very height of achievement, and therefore was beginning to know how little human achievement is. He had long received the fealty of the King of Scotland after a victorious march as far as Abernethy, he was paramount in claim over all Britain: he had overcome the most difficult because the most unexpected of the tasks set to him by fate—the pacification of the realm after his first great victory, and the sporadic anarchy which broke out for years afterwards. But he was not to end in peace. The combined fierceness and weight of his temper remained, and he who (like Charlemagne) had been obese too early, growing now unwieldy with age, yet still maintained his energies intact and could mount and ride in arms till the very end.

He needed so to do. For in the place of men rising against the peace sporadically for local gain, there came feudal rebellion: the greater men under whom all feudal territories were of necessity organized successfully attempted to increase themselves. The son of his nearest and most valued supporter, Fitz Osbern, the younger son who had been given the county of Hereford, Earl thereof, was watching an opportunity to rebel. So was Waltheof, who ruled in the north, and at Northampton and Huntingdon—a man native to England but now one of the great pillars of the new dynasty. So was Ralph, also born here, but of a Breton mother and governing East Anglia, Norfolk and Suffolk, now married to the sister of his fellow-conspirator,

Roger, the Fitz Osbern of Hereford.

These three, Roger, Ralph, Waltheof, thought it possible to return to the conditions of the generation before Hastings, to be rid of the strong central rule and to govern independently each his share of England. Waltheof hung back, even though William's absence in Normandy must have tempted him. Nevertheless when the three rebels were tried in the Christmas Council of 1075, which lasted until the beginning of 1076, while Ralph, having fled, was condemned as contumacious, Roger was only kept within castle bounds. Waltheof seemed to be in greater peril.

William had made it a principle never to shed human blood in the way of justice. There was in his determined character a vein, unique for that time, of what his contemporaries would have thought superstition upon this point—as though he were cleric instead of lay and felt he had no right to play the part of the Almighty and end any man's life by decree. Yet here for Waltheof an exception was made. When the Great Council was held again by Whitsuntide at Westminster he was condemned to death, and after long prison was beheaded, on a Hampshire hill which looks down upon Winchester. Waltheof had been given by William his own niece as wife—she hated him, but William was not of a kind to have listened to a woman's hatred, especially of a younger woman over whom he had authority, and more especially in a matter where his principles had always been so strong. The action is the stranger because an increasing number of Englishmen, especially of the common people, were serving as mercenaries directly under William's command, were sharing in his glories, and were beginning to make of him a popular King—and it was just these men who had most sympathized with Waltheof. When the man had thus been put to death they reverenced him as a martyr. But why? And why should William have done what he did? There seems to be no sufficient answer.

After that strange exceptional date, William went overseas, back into his own land. Odo, ruling for him, was more oppressive than he himself would have been; in the suppression of one rising four years later he put men to death wholesale or bought their lives of them at a price.

William, abroad in these ending years, suffered his first defeat in the field: a small matter, but yet another addition to the burden. He had made a raid into Brittany, he was driven out by the young King of France, Philip, allied with the Breton lord. Then Robert, his elder son, rebelled. It was the usual feudal rebellion, the effort to increase revenue by getting territories from a superior, but it was a rebellion against his own blood, and William received a new wound in the soul. This Robert, William's eldest son, was a man one half of whose character compelled and should compel admiration, but not the other. For he was a true soldier of the time, very active and courageous, risking his short, stout, little bandy-legged body in furious mêlées. He was claiming some advance from the revenues of Normandy and Maine, for his father had promised him that he should be heir to these, and, following the precedent of the Dukes and Kings of the French Duchies, had caused homage to be done to his eldest son during his own life. Robert, certainly in debt, clamored for an advance, and not receiving it fought— exiled himself—wandered about in a sort of knight-errantry— came back to the borders of Normandy and fought again.

What William suffered from this was the more grievous because his wife, upon whom his life and character had reposed, could not forbear from sending secretly the wherewithal of livelihood at least to her eldest son. William reproached her with bitterness, but she maintained her affection for the rebel. In a frontier fighting between him and William under the walls of a castle (now disappeared) called Gerberoi, belonging to the King of France and enfeoffed by him to Robert (the mound on which it stood is still conspicuous), the Duke suffered defeat again.

William had with him his third son, William the younger, nicknamed "Rufus," a strange, unpleasing creature, but the most courageous of them all; and of the English who were there one was the son of that sheriff who had first acknowledged him at Wallingford at the crossing of the Thames after his march round London. Robert in the turmoil reached the horse of his father and those about his father. The Englishman fell. William himself was wounded in the hand by his son's lance and the horse beneath him fell under the blow of an arrow; the now far too heavy figure was thrown to the ground, and it was in saving his lord thus in peril that the Englishman died. The younger William was wounded as well. The whole affair was a defeat, for the Duke's force made off as best it could, leaving Gerberoi untaken.

A peace was made between the son and father, but it did not hold, and Robert spent all the last years of the reign once more in exile—his mother never saw him again—and three years afterwards, in the winter of 1083, that mother died.

She had long been ill. William gave her a great funeral in that Abbey which she had founded over against his own at Caen, and throughout England Masses were said for her soul. This final blow fell after other very grievous ones had fallen. The second son, intermediate between Robert and the younger William, died in the New Forest; his daughter, who had been pledged to an unwished-for marriage, died too: William, with his soul now almost alone in the midst of his millions of subjects and possessions and memories, had still to struggle on; he might not mourn in peace, nor go down to the grave other than under arms.

There was rebellion in Maine, and of one castle a long, long siege. That siege also failed, and William was willing to compromise and to make peace with his own vassal. It was a smallish place that had thus stood out, but the fame of it filled three years of successful resistance—it was Hubert's castle of Ste. Suzanne. The peace between this successful rebel and his defeated lord (for defeated in his object William had been—the place remained intact) was made in England where William then lay. Those last years had been further disturbed by the unceasing and wholly selfish violence of Odo. This younger son of Arletta's, this half-brother, to whom the Duke had given the greatest wealth and power after he had acquired his new realm, had but founded legends of hatred against himself and imperilled all William's scheme of acceptance and consent.

It was a little before Matilda's death that Odo of Bayeux, struck with a sort of madness after such tyranny, conceived a scheme of succeeding to the Papacy. The impossible ambition and the huge disturbance which it meant led, after so much provocation, to the end of the power of Odo of Bayeux; but that Bishop in Council protested his clergy—only the Pope could try him and judge him. William, tutored by Lanfranc, told him in full Council that if he himself laid his hand upon his brother, he thus seized not a Bishop of the Church Universal and immune, but a feudatory of his own—the Governor of Kent.

With his wife dead, the sooner this warring life of his should end, the better for him and his rest.

The old man (for all these fierce years had aged him) after some three years of widowhood mounted again with difficulty his corpulent body and went off in an anger as strong as that of his youth against the border of the Duchy of France to the south, where the tenants of King Philip, his feudal lord, had been raiding. Or perhaps it was a band of Philip's own men, holding the castle of Mantes, who had come north the few miles into Normandy and had looted. There William's answer had been, even so late and after so many difficulties, a determined refusal of their claim to the Vexin, that is, to the disputed Mantes district, lying on the land that separated the overlordship of Rouen from the overlordship of the King of Paris. Young Philip, hearing of the old man coming south, had joked in the hearing of those about him—asking when the child would be born—and William's anger flamed higher than ever. He wasted the land all round, he burnt the houses of the city, he did sacrilege in his fury, for he did not even spare the churches.

He was riding, on the Assumption—15th August 1087—spent with exertion, through the smoldering streets of the conquered and destroyed town, when his horse stumbled and threw his over-weighted figure against the high pommel of the saddle. The blow was more than he could bear; they had to carry him back to his capital down river, to Rouen, a man who now knew he was dying.

They laid him for repose and quietness in the Abbey of St. Gervais, in the suburbs outside the city, and there he lingered through the last two weeks of August and on through the first week of September.

When he found death very near, he was still able to make his dispositions for what was to follow. To Robert, as of hereditary right, as to one also to whom the feudatories had done homage, he left the hereditary Continental land. To his younger son, who had been born in England, Henry, now twenty years old, he left a store of silver (a capital in social value of something like half a million today) and presumably certain lands for his endowment as well.

But the arrangement he made in the matter of England is strange and provokes our thought. He had no doubt whatsoever on his right—he was King of England by a rightful claim and the favor of God, who had confirmed that claim in ordeal by battle—it was his right, without question, to found a new dynasty in that realm. He would not unite it with Robert's Duchy, he did not even actually appoint; what he said was that he dared not dispose, and that, as in the matter of that "last quarter of an hour" at Hastings, God must decide—which meant in effect the Priest upon whose wisdom and authority he had so long and profoundly relied, the great Lanfranc, still towering above all contemporaries there at Canterbury, in his eightieth year. But to Lanfranc he certainly recommended the choice of Rufus, the son who had been most filial, and the one whose evil condition he had not perhaps divined—or if he had, preferred to ignore.

He bade the young man set out for the coast and be ready to sail across the Channel, and indeed, when the news of his father's death came, the younger William sailed at once from near where Deauville now stands, and Lanfranc in England fulfilled the great King's will and saw to it that this son should be crowned.

For William, now lying at St. Gervais, there was nothing left but to die. He made open confession of that which troubled his soul, his acts of violence, and in such violence of wrong; and then in the last hour he had the strength to recommend himself to the Mother of God, by whose prayers he might be reconciled with her Son. And the considerable business of that life was over.

NOTES

NOTES

If you have enjoyed this book, consider making your next selection from among the following . . .

Prices guaranteed through June 30, 1994.

Passion of Jesus and Its Hidden Meaning. Fr. Groenings, S.J........12.50
The Victories of the Martyrs. St. Alphonsus Liguori............... 8.50
Canons and Decrees of the Council of Trent. Transl. Schroeder......12.50
Sermons of St. Alphonsus Liguori for Every Sunday..............16.50
A Catechism of Modernism. Fr. J. B. Lemius.................... 4.00
Alexandrina—The Agony and the Glory. Johnston................. 4.00
Blessed Margaret of Castello. Fr. William Bonniwell............... 6.00
The Ways of Mental Prayer. Dom Vitalis Lehodey.................11.00
Fr. Paul of Moll. van Speybrouck............................. 9.00
St. Francis of Paola. Simi and Segreti.......................... 7.00
Communion Under Both Kinds. Michael Davies................... 1.50
Abortion: Yes or No? Dr. John L. Grady, M.D................... 1.50
The Story of the Church. Johnson, Hannan, Dominica.............16.50
Religious Liberty. Michael Davies............................. 1.50
Hell Quizzes. Radio Replies Press............................. 1.00
Indulgence Quizzes. Radio Replies Press........................ 1.00
Purgatory Quizzes. Radio Replies Press......................... 1.00
Virgin and Statue Worship Quizzes. Radio Replies Press............ 1.00
The Holy Eucharist. St. Alphonsus............................ 8.50
Meditation Prayer on Mary Immaculate. Padre Pio................ 1.25
Little Book of the Work of Infinite Love. de la Touche............. 2.00
Textual Concordance of The Holy Scriptures. Williams............35.00
Douay-Rheims Bible. Leatherbound............................35.00
The Way of Divine Love. Sister Josefa Menendez.................17.50
Mystical City of God—Abridged. Ven. Mary of Agreda.............18.50
Raised from the Dead. Fr. Hebert.............................15.00
Love and Service of God, Infinite Love. Mother Louise Margaret....10.00
Life and Work of Mother Louise Margaret. Fr. O'Connell...........10.00
Autobiography of St. Margaret Mary........................... 4.00
Thoughts and Sayings of St. Margaret Mary..................... 3.00
The Voice of the Saints. Comp. by Francis Johnston............... 5.00
The 12 Steps to Holiness and Salvation. St. Alphonsus............. 7.00
The Rosary and the Crisis of Faith. Cirrincione & Nelson.......... 1.25
Sin and Its Consequences. Cardinal Manning.................... 5.00
Fourfold Sovereignty of God. Cardinal Manning.................. 5.00
Catholic Apologetics Today. Fr. Most.......................... 8.00
Dialogue of St. Catherine of Siena. Transl. Algar Thorold......... 9.00
Catholic Answer to Jehovah's Witnesses. D'Angelo................ 8.00
Twelve Promises of the Sacred Heart. (100 cards)................. 5.00
St. Aloysius Gonzaga. Fr. Meschler...........................10.00
The Love of Mary. D. Roberto................................ 7.00
Begone Satan. Fr. Vogl...................................... 2.00
The Prophets and Our Times. Fr. R. G. Culleton.................11.00
St. Therese, The Little Flower. John Beevers.................... 4.50
St. Joseph of Copertino. Fr. Angelo Pastrovicchi................. 4.50
Mary, The Second Eve. Cardinal Newman....................... 2.50
Devotion to Infant Jesus of Prague. Booklet...................... .75
The Faith of Our Fathers. Cardinal Gibbons.....................13.50
The Wonder of Guadalupe. Francis Johnston..................... 6.00
Apologetics. Msgr. Paul Glenn................................ 9.00
Baltimore Catechism No. 1................................... 3.00

Prices guaranteed through June 30, 1994.

At your bookdealer or direct from the publisher.

Prices guaranteed through June 30, 1994.

ABOUT THE AUTHOR

Hilaire Belloc
1870-1953

The great Hilaire Belloc was likely the most famous and influential Catholic historian of the past two centuries. His rare understanding of the central role of the Catholic Faith in forming Western Civilization—from the time of Christ up to our own—still opens the eyes of many today.

Hilaire Belloc was born in 1870 at La Celle, St. Cloud, France. His father was a distinguished French lawyer; his mother was English. After his father's death, the family moved to England. Hilaire did his military service in France, then returned to Balliol College, Oxford, taking first-class honors in history when he graduated in 1895. It has been said that his ambition was to rewrite the Catholic history of his two fatherlands, France and England. In 1896 he married Elodie Hogan of Napa, California; the marriage was blessed with two sons and two daughters.

During a period of 50 years—until he suffered a stroke in 1946—Hilaire Belloc wrote over a hundred books on history, economics, military science and travel, plus novels and poetry. He also wrote hundreds of magazine and newspaper articles. He served for a time as a member of the English House of Commons and edited a paper called the *Eye-Witness*.

As an historian, Belloc is largely responsible for correcting the once nearly universal *Whig* interpretation of British history, which attributed Britain's greatness to her Anglo-Saxon and Protestant background.

Hilaire Belloc visited the United States several times, giving guest lectures at both Notre Dame and Fordham Universities. Among his most famous books are *The Great Heresies, Survivals and New Arrivals* (something of a sequel to the above), *The Path to Rome, Characters of the Reformation,* and *How the Reformation Happened.* Hilaire Belloc died in 1953, leaving behind a great legacy of insight regarding the true, though largely unrecognized, inspirer of Western Civilization—the Catholic Church.